Baby boo-Boos
Common Mistakes That

All New Dads Make

Guide To Avoiding Typical Mistakes for First-Time & Expectant Fathers
During Pregnancy and First Year

Magnus Moosa

CONTENTS

ARE YOU READY TO BE A NEW DAD?

First-time fatherhood can feel a little overwhelming and stressful, especially if you don't know where to begin or what to expect. Well, the first step that I recommend is to find out how much you currently know about fatherhood.
Take my short New Dad Quiz now to see how much you really know about fatherhood and babies by visiting www.magnusmoosa.com or scanning the QR code below:

INTRODUCTION

A wet diaper means it's time for a change, and the quicker the better. It usually also means that your baby boy's bladder is empty, right? Sadly, it wasn't until the middle of changing my son's diaper–as I was reaching for a clean one–that I found out how wrong that theory was. My son wasn't done peeing.

Except now, he was peeing on *me*. I didn't even have time to dash to grab a towel to block the stream. My son finished his business, gurgled, and gave me a toothless grin as I stood there with a soaked shirt and a new theory on baby's–especially boys'–bladders. After that day, my wife frequently reminded me to keep my mouth closed during diaper changes, usually with a giggle.

A lot of new dads know exactly how it feels to be the incompetent one, if not in the exact same scenario, one very similar to it. Babies don't come with instruction manuals. It's easy to believe common misconceptions and to assume you know what you're doing! In reality, like most first-time dads, you are just trying to fumble your way through it.

Whether you are about to become a dad or you've recently had a child, the only thing you can be sure of is that being a dad to a baby is going to take some getting used to!

Your lack of experience as a father can feel overwhelming. You don't know where to start, and you may not know what to do. All of these unknowns can cause a lot of worry and stress. Worse, they can affect your mental health. Every parent undoubtedly worries about the future and every little thing that might go wrong with their baby, while at the same time worrying about their relationship with their partner or co-parent. There are so many uncertainties that come along with the anticipation of becoming a parent; these uncertainties grow even more so once your baby is born.

Even though you are joining the ranks of parents who are all going through what you are feeling, somehow it's easy to feel like you're going through it alone. But that's why you went looking for a little help from someone who has already been through it...a few times actually.

First of all, be assured: you are absolutely *not alone*.

Second of all, you are perfectly capable of learning all of the things you need to know to be a great dad. You just need a little guidance. That's why you're reading this book. You know, there are many books written for new moms, but not as many for new dads. Having a go-to, all-in-one source, for your questions and ideas on how to navigate through your journey is an invaluable tool.

First-time fathers typically feel like they do not know what fatherhood truly entails, and they often feel like they don't have access to that information. You need to equip yourself with the knowledge to succeed and avoid critical mistakes. And you must be aware of what those mistakes are to watch out for them.

Whether you are a dad-to-be, an uncle, a brother, or a friend, you want to lend your support toward that journey into fatherhood. First-time mothers too frequently have no idea what to expect of the dad, or how to effectively support them in their experience. This book is a guidepost to assist any of the above in their pursuit of fatherly support.

We will explore just about every mistake you might encounter as a new dad, from the standpoint of a very experienced father who's already learned the tricks. Who better to guide you than a loving father of three? My experience will encourage you and lead you around those paternal pitfalls. Together, we will make sure you have all of the tools you need to get excellent results as a parent.

I was not always experienced in fatherhood. Growing up without a father left me with little in the way of how it was supposed to be done or what to expect. It also instilled in me just how painful it can be for a child and the impact not having a dad can have on them growing up.

My journey into fatherhood began at about the same time I started my career in construction. I lived a simple life. I loved football, hanging out with friends, and I was enjoying a healthy relationship with my wife, Sonya.

Then everything changed in one day when I found out she was pregnant. I had to figure out–with no guidance– how to look after my pregnant wife and how to raise our child.

Stress overwhelmed me. Frustration with my lack of knowledge and, in retrospect, my pride got in the way of learning new skills and getting things done effectively.

I worried about financial stability and trying to support my partner, all while putting on a brave face like I knew what I was doing. Inside, I was just anxious. I made many mistakes.

I didn't always take the best care of myself. I wasn't sleeping enough, I was working too hard, and neglecting to eat right all of the time. Then, when the baby was born, I made more mistakes. From buying too many unnecessary baby-centric products, to foolishly worrying about spoiling them by holding them too often. I even made the mistake of holding my baby upright to "stand" and "walk", thinking that it was strengthening their legs, when it was really just exhausting them.

Three years later, I had my second child and found that it was much easier because our first baby had given us a wealth of knowledge as well as hands-on experience. I was able to more readily anticipate the needs of my pregnant wife, and make the second baby's introduction into the family a lot smoother. Little details I stressed about the first time around seemed much less important in the face of the issues I knew really mattered.

By the time I had my third child, being the dad of a newborn was practically a walk in the park. I'd learned exactly what was needed of me and the best ways to navigate the early stages of fatherhood. I want to give this experience to you. Rest assured, my knowledge comes from personal, first-hand experience and wisdom, and from striving to become the best partner and father that I can be.

The love I have for my children, and my passionate, hands-on approach to fathering inspired me to pass on the tools, insights, and hacks to help other new fathers deal with their own journey. I want to help you and the other dads out there avoid the mistakes I made.

Raising a child without guidance is like driving without a map in new territory. Becoming a father can be difficult but you can take action to make things a little easier by preparing and learning from other people's experiences. I've learned that most fathers have common struggles and make the same, mostly typical mistakes that I did.

I have been through what you are going through now, the same worries and uncertainties. I overcame them and learned how to better myself through research and experience.

And I have found the rewards of being a father are beyond measure.

From that first dirty diaper to the hundredth all-night rocking session, to just sitting and staring as your baby sleeps on your chest, there is so much more joy to come than you could ever imagine.

With a little help, you're going to be there for all of it, for your partner and your child. What I need to do first is teach you how to manage all of those things, good and bad, prepare and inform you, so that you can take them in stride and actually get to enjoy the challenges along the way without feeling like you're drowning in diapers. But I'll get into those sticky situations–so to speak–in a bit.

As you begin to understand what it means to be a dad, I hope you will discover the wonders of having a child just as I did, increasing your confidence and competence as a man, partner, and father.

One of the first things you will have to address as a first-time father is emotions and learning how to regulate them. You have to gain control of yourself when dealing with your child and handling parenting situations. Frustration and impatience will be two of your most common hurdles as you begin your role as a dad...

1

GO WITH THE FLOW, IMPATIENCE, AND FRUSTRATION

The frustrations of first-time parenthood are real. Exhaustion can make you impatient and irritable and will test your connection to your child. First-time fathers can sometimes be impatient and frustrated when things don't go to plan. They're used to working on their own schedule and doing things a certain time-effective, or even just selfish, routine way. After all, up until now, you may have made a few accommodations for your partner, and you've expected your partner to make accommodations for you.

Babies don't know how to work on anyone's schedule but their own, and plans? Forget about them. You're going to need to learn to roll with it.

If you don't, it will often be too easy to find yourself raising your voice and getting angry or impatient, and you will feel like a bad dad for losing your patience. That doesn't mean you can't work on it daily, learn from your mistakes, and practice steps to avoid it happening as much as possible.

Learning self-regulation and techniques for managing your stress and emotions will prevent you from making these mistakes with your baby. The last thing you want to do is take out your frustrations on your child.

Just a Baby - Losing your temper with your child

We all reach the end of our rope at times and want to shout and vent our anger. It's completely human and natural. And as much as you love your child, their crying will wear on you after a while. You'll be frustrated by your inability to determine whatever is wrong and how to fix it. Combine that with the lack of sleep caused by a baby's erratic sleeping and eating (and pooping) schedule, and you'll lose the stamina to endlessly put up with more stress. There will be times you'll want to beg your baby to sleep and to just be quiet. But, just as you wouldn't shout in your boss's face over your frustrations at work because you know it will only end poorly, and ultimately it's wrong, you must learn how to mitigate and manage your emotions around your baby. Everyone hates regretting an outburst that you know you could have avoided.

Until you screw up and lose your cool, you need to remember that there is no one at fault between you and your fussy baby. Frustration is normal. But giving in to the resulting anger can have worse repercussions than you feeling like a jerk. Accidents happen, especially when you get out of hand.

There's a very good reason they sometimes show you the 'baby shaking' video at the hospital. All of us are horrified and it really seems ridiculous to have to inform parents about the risks of jostling and aggressive handling…but it happens. We all agree it is wrong, but you can make a snap decision and make a terrible mistake resulting in permanent injury, or worse, death. These warnings may seem a bit grim, but raising your little one is serious business, despite the wondrous happiness and laughter you will all share through it.

Harmful actions aside, the good news is that even if you have those not-so-good days when you simply growl your angst for sweet sweet silence, the good days will outshine the bad. When you are sleep-deprived everything seems too big. It's crucial to remind yourself who you are and that you love your baby. It doesn't make you a bad parent.

What you do need to do is teach yourself some techniques and plan some strategies to handle your emotions. It's okay to have bad days and believe me, you will have them! Sleep deprivation and stress are inevitable. Feeling overwhelmed and helpless to do anything is also inevitable. Know that feeling angry and impatient doesn't make you a bad parent. You're human! You're going to feel that way. But you need to know how to handle your emotions in a good way to be a good parent. That's why this section is so important for you to read.

A lot of people think that they will become someone else entirely once their child is born. Now, this is true in some ways. You won't believe or comprehend how you feel about your kid until they arrive. There's nothing like it. However, you have to keep your expectations realistic. You're still you!

The stakes seem so very high. You don't get days off from this new life. But don't get dragged down into despair. Don't set yourself up for failure by blowing the severity of your situation up to astronomical proportions. Ultimately, be kind and forgiving to yourself, or you will seed resentment toward yourself and your child.

Just take a deep breath. Think about what you are about to do or yell. Then go grab a pillow and shut yourself in the closet and shout into the pillow. Your baby will stay occupied crying in their crib for thirty seconds. Let it out. Then head back in.

Use preconceived techniques to de-escalate your anxieties. Stepping away or stepping outside can be the breath of fresh air you need to sidestep a less-than-proud moment. And we mean, literally, outside. Sometimes we don't realize how trapped we feel being cooped up indoors most of our days.

Be honest with yourself and your partner if you have to take a break for a bit. Take turns with the hard stuff. Give each other breaks.

Find your anchor in logic and problem-solving. Why is your baby acting this way? Check off the possibilities to narrow in on the solution to fix the issue for both of you. They can't do anything for themselves, it's up to you.

At the end of the day, always let it go and love. Allowing love to be the motivation for all of your actions and the filter for your behavior will keep your frustration in check. Your baby will react to your mood and feelings, and you can't stay mad at that cute little face!

Crocodile Tears - Taking Crying Personally

To your baby, you are a fuzzy shape that solves their problems. Crying is their way of telling you that they need you to do something. Crying does not mean "I hate you." Many parents suffer from the misplaced guilt of a constantly crying baby.

Much like the criticism, we will discuss shortly and the frustration of not understanding how to get your screaming newborn to comply, you must remember that there is no malice in your baby's tears. They're not mad at you, sad, or grieving like an older human. Those are developed and learned emotional connotations. They may be in pain or discomfort, sure, but there is nothing personal in it. They don't have that capacity yet!

Furthermore, they might even just be bored or over-stimulated.

Crying is just their way of sharing feelings and communicating, and babies' feelings are not very complex. Try not to fabricate an offense from someone who can't survive without you. And when you just can't handle it, tag your partner in and take a breather.

STRESS MANAGEMENT

We all have to unwind, regardless of whether we are parents or life-long bachelors! Besides, don't you want to be known as the cool, level-headed dad?

We've come up with a list of some solid suggestions for you to address the stress. Get in the practice of using them and managing your concerns now, before you're dropped into daddy-dom. Successful implementation of healthy processing capabilities will work wonders in the short and long term. Get creative and add your own twists to this list; nobody knows what works best to unwind better than you do. You've got this.

Better Out Than In - Talking About It

Talk it out. We don't often realize how much putting words to our feelings helps expunge them from our minds. Share your woes with someone you know who will listen to you; a friend, a relative, a coworker. If you see a therapist, that's exactly what you go to them for, so use that time to work through things and get past them. Don't keep that baggage in your closet at home.

Sometimes, it even helps to simply say it out loud to yourself. Who else could understand your frustrations better than you? Taking a few minutes alone in the car before coming home to recap the day and unload the junk can spare you having to carry it into the house with you.

Garbage In, Garbage Out - Eating Healthy

Eating right has to be one of the most integral parts of feeling good and functioning. It seems self-evident, but we have complicated relationships with our food. Food makes us feel good, not only for sustenance but the associations of pleasure in our brains. The catch is that repeated use of treats just to feel better leads to all sorts of physical issues. Keep healthy snacks around for when you need to munch.

Unhealthy junk food ultimately perpetuates your stress by running down your body. The growing field of nutritional psychiatry is studying the effects of food on our moods. In the simplest terms, what they are discovering is that most of the receptors for chemicals that make us feel good are found in the gut. In other words, getting frustrated and feeling bad is directly related to hunger and poor diet. Inflammation and an upset in the balance of good bacteria in your stomach from highly processed foods can lead to long-term side effects like depression and diseases like diabetes (Naidoo, 2019).

The Best Medicine

Laughter is the most useful means of making your entire day better. Try smiling for thirty seconds sometimes when you aren't feeling your best. They say that even though you know you're faking it, so to speak, it can sort of trick your brain into shifting your mood. And you'll probably laugh at yourself for your fake smile when you do it, which starts the cycle toward feeling so much better. And if that fails, put on some puppy videos, or watch someone slip and slide down their icy driveway in their bunny slippers. Humor and distractions will get you back on your feet and grinning in no time.

Tea'd Off

Many varieties of tea boast calming characteristics, so brew yourself a cup to soothe your daily preoccupation. The act of sitting still and taking a quiet moment to stop and sip your hot tea can clear your head and bring you back to center.

Mind the Gap - Staying Mindful

Being mindful can serve to give you purpose and minimize stress. Mindfulness is practiced awareness of the here and now, of how we are feeling and experiencing what is happening to us. Too often, we keep a speeding raceway of wayward thoughts and worries barreling through our heads. Try some simple techniques to focus on being present:

- Breathe deeply and evenly. Focus on your breathing for a bit. Good breathing habits can even lower your blood pressure!
- Close your eyes, without dozing off, and just be still for a few minutes.
- Stop the noise. Find a quiet place for a micro-vacation from the "busy-busy".
- Fixate on something simple you are doing. Make a list of the things you want to do and need to do, and put your whole focus into that one task before moving on to the next thing.

Using some of these ideas will come in handy in the future with your baby. The time will fly by regardless of whether you are paying attention or not. Learn how to be present and immersed in those moments so you never forget them.

Physical Exercise

Our days are full. That probably means you aren't getting as much physical activity as you need. Work in some push-ups, sit-ups, and a quick jog. The better shape you can be in by the time the baby comes, the better equipped physically you'll be to endure the tough days. Additionally, exercise is the primary method recommended by physicians to lead a stress-free life. There's a whole bunch of chemistry and biology to back that up, but all you need to know is that doing it will help you!

Not to mention that if you can establish a sound schedule of staying fit now, you stand a better chance of maintaining your workouts through the birth and early years. It's hard to introduce new routines in the hustle and bustle of a baby.

The Rest is Rest

Sleep is at the head of the trifecta of fitness. Eat right, exercise, and sleep. Make the effort to turn in a little earlier some nights to get that extra shut-eye.

Cut the screen time on your devices an hour before bed to promote your brain's natural shut-down procedures. You'll notice how effective the extra rest is and how much more easily you fall asleep.

"THAT WAS HARSH" - TAKING CRITICISM TOO PERSONALLY

"Um, you put the baby's gown on backward. Again."

For some of us, that comment above sounds a lot more like, "Can't you do anything right? You are a terrible father."

How many of us handle criticism well in any area of our lives? How much worse will you handle it when it's directed at your new identity as a father? Dad criticisms are some of the most hurtful and debilitating commentaries that a man can hear. You need to either use it or lose it.

Use It - Turning Criticism into Positivity

First of all, don't listen to that insecurity, and do not beat yourself up. You wouldn't torture yourself over forgetting to buy bread at the store on your way home. So don't torture yourself over the small hiccups with your baby.

Criticism will come at you from all sorts of angles in the next few years, directed at your duty and your role, and how you perform it. Navigating some of it will make you a much better father, while other bits will just eat you up and make you want to never change your baby in public again! Just remember, you can always improve. You can always try again.

Remember that there is GOOD criticism too! Take those things to heart and be willing to listen and accept them to be a better father. Using the good critiques you get, or even finding useful meanings in the negative comments, can turn those harmful jabs into constructive growth.

Criticism Prevention

Everyone has something to say about everything. Although you cannot completely eliminate criticism, you can minimize the opportunities for it.

In tandem with organization and planning, employing stress managing techniques will guide you through the mire of emotional frustrations. Sufficient sleep and good eating habits will keep you from boiling over. Pausing before retorting to snide remarks and taking a deep breath can save you the hassle of defending yourself, or overreacting those times when you are in fact wrong.

Rough and Tough - Most Common Criticisms

Dads get a bad rap. According to a June 2019 C.S. Mott Children's Hospital's Mott Poll Report (2019), the most criticized aspects of being a dad are:

- Too rough.
- Not enough attention to the child.
- Too much discipline.
- Poor diet, mismanaging the children's nutrition. It can be easy to want to be the 'fun' parent (C.S. Mott Children's Hospital, 2019).

Joking aside, these are very serious concerns for dads and how they are viewed. These are the things they have to hear and carry around with them. It can be very defeating, and an all-too-common response is for a lot of fathers to check out and give up. 1 in 5 fathers say they've felt like being less involved because of discouraging and sharp criticism (C.S. Mott Children's Hospital, 2019).

67% of fathers report discipline as the most frequently criticized area of their parenting (C.S. Mott Children's Hospital, 2019). Discipline can be a tough one for dads. We are supposed to follow the law in the house according to many traditions, or we want to behave like the head of our family. This promotes the idea of the man being the aggressive parent, the one who has to be the bad guy. So a lot of dads rebel and try to be their kid's best friend instead, which we all know is not fair to the other parent or the children.

Another wounding assumption about many dads is that fathers are automatically less knowledgeable about their children and not as nurturing.

Statistics also state that at least half of all fathers have been criticized about their parenting choices, most often by their partners which leads to possible hostility in the home (C.S. Mott Children's Hospital, 2019).

Home Team Disadvantage - Being Hostile with Your Partner

The predominant source of criticism is inevitably going to come from your partner. Living situations vary, but it makes sense if you live in close quarters and spend the bulk of your time with each other and your child. This can lead to tensions in your relationship and in how you are raising your baby. How you communicate with each other is key.

Unfortunately, when it comes to communication, men lean toward tendencies to bottle things up. If this is something you struggle with, you will do yourself a huge favor by working on your emotional conditioning and sharing your feelings and stress with your partner.

Stepping back from your affronts for a moment, the two of you will receive criticism as a parenting unit, as well. There are so many cultural and ingrained things that prescribe or assume what your roles should be and how you should raise your kids. Media, society, your circle of friends, or your religious community all proffer a construct of stereotypes, but this is your family!

Grain of Salt - Getting Defensive

Take each other's suggestions seriously, and do your best not to take criticism as an attack. And watch how you offer your own suggestions. Most importantly, spend time together with your newborn as they grow to establish how you want to behave and make decisions together about everything. Teamwork makes the dream work!

Criticism management:

- Practice communicating in a healthy way to avoid fostering resentment.
- Be firm when you think something is unfair; you are an equal partner and get a say.
- Each of you has the right to explain your point of view. It's a two-way street.
- Take all criticism and do something with it. Be constructive within yourself and use every tip to be better, even when it rankles.
- Weigh the source. Most comments will come from people who have no skin in the game. Don't let their remarks make you insecure.
- Take well-meant tips graciously.

Finally, where your partner and the other parent of your baby are concerned, just be there for them even when you feel unneeded. Appreciate each other and decide that you are going to enjoy even the uncomfortable times.

WHAT A RUSH - RUSHING THROUGH YOUR CHILD'S BABY MOMENTS

Speaking of enjoying things, time flies and before long you'll be looking back and wondering where it all went. Parents are always shaking their heads at new moms and dads and warning them about how fast kids grow up, but it's impossible to appreciate until you experience it first-hand. Your kids will progress so much in just three to six months. With infants it's exponential. Your swaddled bundle will master entire skill sets in a matter of days as they grow in the first year.

Be wary of rushing your baby into their next stage without taking the time to both enjoy the moment and let them revel in their achievements.

Above all else, make a point to spend as much time with them as possible. Drive them nuts with how many photos you take of every minute, every event, and milestone. Just don't forget to be in those pictures with them too sometimes! You're making and documenting memories that you will share with them in stories as they grow, the legends, and the tall tales. Those stories are their history. It's your gift to them and your legacy.

Being your best and facilitating your availability to your child will come down to you staying on top of your duties and monitoring your behavior. One of the biggest factors in your success for all of these things will be good time management and discipline to establish a routine. Next, we will discuss how to put organization into practice for optimal parenting.

Takeaway Tips:

- It's OK to get frustrated. Step back and take a breath.
- Do things you love. Don't neglect your hobbies.
- Crying babies aren't mad at you. They only have one way of communicating their needs to you through crying.
- Ask for help to avoid mishaps, stress-related fumbles, or losing your cool.
- Practice patience. And remember that patience takes practice.
- Find your triggers and how you control and avoid them. You're in charge.
- Criticism is just commentary. You choose how to interpret and apply it.
- You're the parent, too. And you are a team. Discuss rather than criticize.
- Appreciate your partner. Appreciate yourself.
- Take your time. Enjoy and savor being a dad.

2

MESSAGE TO MANAGEMENT, ROUTINE AND TIME

No matter how much time you think you have to get ready, there will never quite be enough to get it all done. When your child arrives, your routine will change drastically.

Many new dads tend to underestimate the importance of careful time management and setting up a system of reminders to help them complete their daily tasks. Time management and routine are the most important things for you to establish around your new baby to keep you all stable. We aren't talking about watching the clock every minute, but a system that allows you to manage all the things you need to do, and provides time for you to be able to do the things you want to do, as well. Organization, anticipating hurdles, and planning ahead of time will all be instrumental skills to develop in your new role.

Bedtime Business - Not Having a Bedtime Routine

As a soon-to-be parent, it's up to you to make the hard calls and discipline not only yourself but also set down protocols for your family to thrive within. Your new schedule may be a bit inconsistent, but the one thing you have to stay firm on is bedtime.

Staying up late happens, sometimes for fun, more often out of necessity or mismanaged time. You may think, I can stay up after I put the baby down for the night and get a few things done. Almost without a single exception, this is a bad idea. Weigh the cost.

You need to sleep as much as your child does.

While doing some things you enjoy does help to ease tension and make you function better, sleep needs to take priority over fun. At least right at first, until you find you become accustomed to your duties as a dad. Sometimes it is all too tempting to just watch one more episode of your favorite show but you will be kicking yourself for not taking advantage of sleeping when your little one gets sick and needs you three nights in a row... all night. A well-rested man makes a better, more efficient father. And you'll enjoy your limited me-time more when you don't feel exhausted.

Time's A'wasting - Not Managing Your Time Properly

This brings us to a similar topic that includes bedtime and all of the rest. Establishing reasonable time management skills in your life will help you wrangle your wayward habits and sleeping hurdles. Organization and planning will make you a more effective parent and set you up for success.

Best Laid Plans - Not Planning Ahead

Not planning is one of the biggest stressors that will seriously hurt your productivity as a new father. A lack of organization will have you scrambling to get out the door, so stay ready and think a step ahead. Your partner has enough on their plate without waiting for you to get your act together!

Set your clothing out the night before, and get a spare baby bag ready. When you have a little downtime, do yourself a favor and pre-prep a couple of days out! Think of it as meal planning. And on that note, meal prep, too! All of these are excellent tools to consolidate your tightly scheduled days. Help the future-you be a champ!

Stay ready. Whenever possible keep on top of the laundry, and the chores, but also prioritize what needs to get done. Cleaning out the garage can probably wait.

ER - Have an emergency plan. IF for ANY reason you had to run out in the middle of the night or day, you don't want to be scrambling for essentials in a panic. Keep a "night bag" packed in the hall closet or better yet, in the trunk of the car. This should include all of your needs and the kids' things.

- A change of clothing for each of you.
- Extra toothbrushes and toiletries.
- Contact info in case you have no cell service and have to use a landline.
- First aid kit.
- Flashlight.
- FUN. Diversions for the children. You may need to distract them and keep them busy.

Take the time to think through anything else you may need in a crisis. We know, this sounds scary and stressful, but you will be so much better equipped for emergencies big and small if you think ahead. Even if it's a minor thing like dropping the baby off at a sitter's last minute.

Not Organizing

Planning is paramount, and putting it down in writing will keep it organized! Make lists. Leave yourself notes. Make a calendar for the family and put it somewhere you all can see it and use it. You can't rely on your memory to get it all done.

Some other tips for keeping your household running smoothly:

- Putting things back where they go will save you lots of headaches.
- Make copies. Multiple copies. Of everything. Create a system of folders and files for documents and important forms. Make one for each child and make duplicates. Ask your mother-in-law to keep some backups for you if need be, whatever you need to do!
- Consolidate the systems you come up with to keep it neat and uncluttered.
- Write it DOWN. All of it.
- Containers and baskets. This one can help mom feel less overwhelmed. Place a toy bin, bookshelf, or basket in every room for baby's junk! It can overrun your home if you're not careful. No one likes to step on a loud squeaky or a sharp building block on their way to the kitchen for a glass of water during the night.

Multi-Task - This is more or less a branch off of organizing and planning. We don't mean you have to learn how to juggle or stretch yourself too thin. The goal here is the opposite! Work tasks into your day when you have small intervals and combine activities when you can. Do you have to wait at the doctor's or the auto shop? Bring things you can get done. In the future, this might mean helping the kids with their homework or even just laying out your week. Any time you have to take a phone call, use a headset and keep working on the dishes to consolidate.

Adjacently, find profitable trade-offs and compromises on day to day. If you can, try to spend the money to have someone else fix the faulty light switch in the basement. Settle for the store-bought treat when you don't have time for baking. This will free you up to focus on the things only you can do.

Hand in hand with multi-tasking is **assessing** where you can cut the fat. What habits are eating up your hours? Do you have any 'time sucks'? Is there any wasted time you can repurpose into other areas? Think of ways you can redirect downtime toward your baby and partner to make all of your lives a little smoother. Try to dial down the idle YouTubing and social media scrolling for now.

That brings us to a gentle suggestion regarding **devices**. Turn them off every now and again. The TV, the tablet, the laptop. Especially if it is a work thing eating into family time. This ties back into compartmentalizing and preventing too much bleed from one area of your life into the next.

Make Extra - Whatever you're making or doing, cooking, cleaning, or planning, leave some leftovers for more projects, replace what you used, saving some prepared food ready in the fridge for any eventuality. If you can knock out all of the laundry in one go, get it done! Any time you can, save yourself as much hassle as possible by using the 'quick' method. Don't leave yourself a mountain of dishes to do, but also think about what can be left unfinished and still work, like folding every piece of laundry.

Exercise - Getting moving and breaking a sweat will help your mental state and make the daunting stress manageable. And you can even multitask while you do it. Take the kids with you in the stroller, or put them out in the yard while you get your reps in. A healthy and fit dad will keep up with the kids a lot better. Besides, the kids need activity too, and you will be bonding at the same time! You may miss the luxury of the gym for a while, but you can still meet your needs.

Not Prioritizing

You have to get everything done! We know it feels that way sometimes. However, tasks do have levels of importance. Long-term house projects can be placed on the back burner for the time being. Washing underwear when you are down to your last pair of socks probably sits somewhere upward of the middle, whereas the near-empty bag of diapers and baby formula cannot wait.

Bracket your days and tasks into relative chunks. It doesn't have to be an itemized list, just generalized. Of course, allow leeway for changes, but set out a time for each thing that needs doing, and that you want to get done.

You are much more likely to get something done when you put a date and time to it.

Prioritizing will inevitably lead to streamlining your life and processes. Unfortunately, some stuff has to get cut out, but better that you make that call than time making it for you at the expense of things you wish you could have done.

Now, given the nature of how important your baby is, you will be inclined to put everything baby-related at the top of the list and everything YOU as an afterthought. This won't do. Leave available moments, or even the odd evening off for 'you-time. This means without kids some of the time. Don't overlook the importance of alone time, as well. We all need a bit of quiet time to recharge our energies and our patience. Everyone will benefit if dad is at his best.

Not Taking Advantage of Remote Work Opportunities

Work from home when you can. In this day and age, especially in the last couple of years, remote working is so much more common and acceptable. Many companies are more than willing to work with you on it if you take the time to ask. Use this to your advantage to be more available to your family. This also might alleviate some of your babysitting costs. Your partner will appreciate it, too. Additionally, treat family time with as much or more importance than work time. Learning when to say no at work will be saying yes to being there for your loved ones. Besides that, you have a baby! Don't bite off more than you can chew.

LEARNING CURVE - NOT USING EVERY RESOURCE AVAILABLE

Despite any possible feelings of inadequate knowledge or skills at being a dad, you have more supportive materials available than ever before. The nurses will be a great source of information once your baby is born, but the more you see it and practice, the more prepared you'll be for the real deal.

Use the Internet. Watch tutorials on how to change diapers, and how to hold your baby. Blogs, articles, and videos can be your crash-course salvation for those nagging details and technical queries you will run into with so many odds and ends as a parent. Nowadays there is a guide for just about anything you could think of. You don't have to wing it.

Additionally, learn the things mom is learning so you stay up to speed. Make pregnancy your responsibility as well. Look into the information that she hasn't learned and really bring something to the table to uphold your end of the deal!

At the end of the day, you want to be able to flop down and close your eyes knowing you checked as many things off your list as you could, and got to enjoy a little bit of it in the meantime. The sense of accomplishment will just be the added satisfaction of the relief that comes with not feeling completely behind. Some days it won't all work out. Don't worry, we've all been there as parents, and once you've slept, tomorrow will start over with all of the opportunities you need to get it right.

BABYSITTERS - YOU'RE NOT HIRING JUST EXTRA HELP

One mistake that is easy to make is overlooking babysitters as a valuable resource. Hiring a helping hand can be a very useful addition to your organization and time management. Never let a good sitter get away.

Even if it's just a friend or family member that offers every now and then, set the time and night and make it a regular occurrence. It's all too easy to never get around to it, for them, and for you. Take advantage of any time you can get a night off guaranteed.

Benefits of a Sitter or Nanny

Having more helping hands will make things more malleable. You have appointments and obligations. Having more help, hired or volunteered will get you to all the other things you need to do, and some that you want to do. As an added bonus, a babysitter can often help out around the house. They may be a paid member of the team, but a team member nonetheless. Clearly set their duties and what they are willing to help with when you hire them (Taylor, 2020).

Partner time - You need time to maintain and work on your marriage or partnership. Time with your child as a family is absolutely imperative in this regard, but you still have your own adult relationship that needs time and effort.

Alternatives - Daycare isn't always the best option for your needs and it can be stressful for children. A daycare associate may have several kids to watch. Babysitting is focused on your child. This can be extra beneficial if your child has any special needs. At home, they have their food, their toys, naps are comfortable, and they can get outside in their own environment that you know is safe. Having them at home also cuts down on preparation, leaving early, and driving risks.

Exposure - Socializing your child with someone other than yourself and your partner opens them up to new experiences and forces them to learn how to behave around other adults and people in general. Your sitter can schedule play dates and other activities where you aren't around as a safety blanket all the time.

Safety and Reliability - Finding someone who you trust will add a level of security to your family life. You can't assume grandparents or aunts and uncles will want to be full-time sitters once you go back to work. You need someone who does this for you. This will keep your family from becoming resentful of assumed help and you from taking advantage unintentionally.

Cost - Hiring a babysitter can seem daunting and out of your price range. This is a common misconception. Look into finding a sitter and the options it opens up for you.

Things to consider when dealing with your sitter:

- Try to keep several sitters on the 'trusted list' in case of cancellations.
- They aren't that expensive. Unless you need daily care at a good rate, they are usually better than daycare for the price.
- Multiple children. Daycares do not offer special rates for more than one kid. Additionally, most sitters will work nights and can stay overnight in some cases, when daycares are not open. Your job might need this special circumstantial attention. The same goes for part-time jobs with inconsistent schedules.
- Babysitters can organize activities to entertain and teach your children instead of sending them to camps and events. They might also take your child to an event you don't like to go to.
- Sitters are ready to cover you on a sick day, whether it's you or your child. Most people cannot skip work to stay home with a sick kid.

Babysitters offer so many auxiliary benefits like: help with homework, unusual bath times when your child gets messy, regular updates, and check-ins with you. They can assist with potty training, allergy management, and exposure, keeping an eye on your house and deliveries for safety, and keeping pets company.

EVERYBODY NOW! - NOT GETTING THE FAMILY INVOLVED

Whoever is over hanging out can contribute. If you ask them nicely, of course. As the old saying goes, "it takes a village." Friends and extended family are your network of problem-solving and emotional support.

This all comes down to asking for help and giving it in return. To be successful, you must build a supportive environment through trusting and mutual relationships, trading favors with neighbors and friends to swap babysitting duties, or even yard work and errands.

Family Ties - Not Setting Boundaries

Dealing with family and babysitting involves carefully established boundaries. You have expectations that they need to be informed of, and they will have some of their own. While you are the parent, they are also doing you a favor. Some discrepancies can come up as a result.

Expectations - Discuss your expectations ahead of time and after the fact to make changes and adjustments. Never correct your babysitter in front of the child. This extends to dislikes and preferences your child might bring to your attention. You should let them know about the complaints or needs, but not in a way that compromises the sitter's relationship with your child (Zmuda, 2015). Be clear and thorough with your desires. This includes TV and digital viewing, books, and any other form of entertainment or activity.

Rules - Set a list of parameters. There should be consequences for not adhering to your requests and they need to be enforced. The most important thing is to remain consistent and communicative.

Location - Agree on where the sitting will happen, and try to have them come to your residence if possible. If they must sit your child somewhere else, even a relative's home, do a walk-through so you are comfortable with it and can mitigate any safety issues. This includes any pets they may have and how your child will interact with them.

Outings - Ask that they get permission from you to take your child on an outing. Family members might assume they can take them wherever if you aren't clear. List your safety expectations and requirements if leaving the house.

- Leave instructions for food and your baby's normal routine, bedtime, etc. Write these out step by step.
- Educate your sitter on the needs and specifics of medicines and allergies, never assume they'll know all the causes and triggers of your baby's special needs.
- Make a quick reference list for them to use. You live your preferences daily with your child. They cannot be expected to remember everything you do.
- Make sure you come home on time, if not early. Show your appreciation for their assistance (Zmuda, 2015).

DIRTY DEEDS - NOT TAKING CARE OF A MESSY DIAPER

More than the unpleasant odors and even your crying child, you have to tend to a heavy diaper sooner than later because leaving a nappy full too long can lead to a whole mess of additional problems. Procrastinating won't just upset your baby, it might cause them to get an infection or rash.

You're never going to like changing diapers. There's nothing fun about handling full nappies. Nevertheless, you have to, and your giggling baby will make all of it worthwhile. Neglect will cause your baby to be very unhappy, and when they're unhappy, you are too.

Dampening Your Spirits

First, we'll cover peeing. This is the most frequent type of mess.

Ever walked home in the rain and not been able to change for a few hours? Now imagine if the rain was urine. You get the idea. Your baby may not have the cognitive reasoning or conditioned distaste for waste, but they have delicate skin and feel yucky just the same.

Leaving wetness against their skin will give them a diaper rash. The same goes for a messy bottom. It's inevitable that they will get it here and there, and you're not a failure as a parent when it happens. Just think about how many times a day they pee and you wipe them. Under those conditions, it's very difficult to completely prevent dry, irritated skin. When diaper rash does pop up, make sure and change them even more frequently and swap out your wipes for a wet washcloth and pat them dry to avoid rubbing and more chafing until the rash heals.

We know the idea of more changes means more money. However, rationing your diapers and trying to make them last is not as economical as you might think. The money you think you're saving will follow those nappies into the bin when your little one gets an infection and has to go see the pediatrician. It's so much better to just change those diapers, as often as you need to.

Speaking of frequency, breastfeeding is an inexact science. Babies nurse as much as they need in order to accommodate growth spurts; the inconsistency of input makes it hard to predict the output. But tracking how many diapers are typical for your baby should give you a good idea of how frequently you'll need to make changes and when to look for full luggage.

Leaks will happen, either due to an excess of urine, or a faulty diaper. If the leaks happen during the day, more than likely you need to change more often. At night time, consider upgrading to a bigger diaper size for more absorbency, or specially designed night diapers. You don't want to be waking a blissfully sleeping baby for changes. If they get uncomfortable, they will let you know in no uncertain terms.

Oh, and an expert tip when changing —always keep a little washcloth or towel over your little boy's 'fire hose' to avoid getting doused while you're trying to situate him!

On the flip side, you'll have to deal with far more unpleasant offerings. It may make you grumpy, but just think about how your baby feels. Just like a wet nappy, you really don't want them waiting with a full, dirty diaper. The consequences for both of you could be very uncomfortable or harmful to your child.

The most common woes and ailments that come from the darker side of the diaper include:

Rashes - Acidic food means acidic poop which means diaper rash. Dry skin from too much wiping can lead to chafing and irritation, cracking, and bleeding. The best way to avoid it is gentle maintenance and getting to wet or dirty nappies as quickly as possible to keep the waste from sitting against your baby's sensitive skin for long.

Yeast infections - Leaving a diaper on too long can lead to developing itchy skin, discharge, and in some cases blisters on the skin. Learn to identify the issue and seek your doctor's advice on how best to treat this infection.

Bladder infections - The main symptom is a burning sensation when peeing. These infections are caused by fecal matter entering the urinary tract. Girls are especially susceptible, so try to keep poop away from the vaginal opening.

Blowout - When a diaper breaks and the beads inside give way, or when the diaper cannot hold anymore, and you get overflow.

Staph infection - Bacteria from poop can get into a rash or sore.

There are many scenarios you will encounter when dealing with your baby's most necessary clothing item. Knowing all of these things will help you stay ahead of the mess, or at least recognize it and minimize your poopoo panics. The two most important tactics are pretty simple:

- Get to it quickly.
- Clean and change them properly every time.

As Below, So above - Not bringing extra diapers or clothes

It's a hot day...You've been traveling and there's no way to turn back now. You have places to be. But then you smell it. And it's exactly what you think it is.

We may as well get most of the gross-out of the way in this first chapter. Yeah, that means getting into vomit and diarrhea. If you're lucky, you won't have to deal with either very often, but when you do, it's imperative that you always have extra diapers and clothes and that you know what you are looking at, how to recognize when it's a problem, and what to do about it.

Oh, and be sure to check your clothes and surfaces for 'sick-up' and other baby fluids. Your hygiene is just as important as theirs.

Both vomiting and diarrhea can occur without your baby being sick. It happens from all sorts of causes and it rarely indicates something serious. More often you can monitor them at home until it passes. The quick list of things to do when either happens is to make sure you keep them clean and feed them a bit more to prevent dehydration as they're losing fluids faster.

Of course, if they have a fever, or are showing splotchy skin and cool extremities, trust your instincts and get to the doctor. Signs of dehydration include:

- Slow or low responsiveness, lethargy.
- Irritability.
- Less urine output.
- Pale or mottled skin.
- Cold extremities.

Bacterial infections can be treated with antibiotics. Viruses, unfortunately, will always have to simply run their course, but the hospital can give them an I.V. tube to stave off dehydration by feeding them liquids, sugars, and salts intravenously.

Now let's finish up with the poop before talking about the puke. As we all know, sometimes diarrhea can just hit us from a little food poisoning, or any number of other mundane reasons. It's the same with your child. You should only be concerned if symptoms of diarrhea:

- Lasts longer than 7 days.
- The child begins to show signs of dehydration
- If it's getting worse, not better.
- High temperature for prolonged periods.
- Blood or mucus in poop.
- Severe abdominal pain.

Otherwise, it will clear up and your little diaper filler will be back to 'regular' shortly. Stay observant of your baby's stool qualities so that you have a good idea of what is normal. You don't have to keep a log, but you need to know the difference between normal and not.

Vomiting

To start with, telling the difference between vomit and spitting up is critical to assessing your baby's state.

Spitting up, also called 'reflux', is extremely common. Your baby's esophagus, the muscular tube to the stomach, is still developing which can cause this spitting up or 'positing'. Otherwise, this could be a sign of milk intolerance or allergies that can cause some regurgitation, but again, not necessarily actual vomiting.

As far as allergies go with milk or food, symptoms should be noticeable very soon after ingestion in the form of swelling around the eyes, an itchy rash, or occasionally vomiting. Gastroenteritis, the common tummy bug, could be a culprit, or food poisoning from bacteria on unsterilized teats and bottles. Always follow the instructions on the formula recipe, as well.

Causes of vomiting:

- Gastroenteritis.
- Allergies/Intolerances.
- Chest infection.
- UTI (Urinary tract infection)
- Middle ear infections.
- Meningitis. (immune response)
- Poison or medicine. (if you know it was poison go straight to the ER)

When to worry and seek help:

- Vomit lasting longer than 2 days.
- Projectile vomiting, severe vomiting expelled heavily.
- Greenish or yellow color (bile), or bloody.
- Refusing to feed.
- Constant vomit, can't keep anything down.
- Stiff neck and rash.

Trust your gut. If you feel uneasy, call your doctor. Better safe than sorry.

We understand the pressures of parenthood can feel insurmountable some days. Take a deep breath and listen up, because that is exactly what we need to discuss in the next chapter.

Takeaway Tips:

- You're not babysitting, you are parenting. You cannot always be the 'fun one'.
- If you have got a phobia of diapers and poop… get over it quick!
- You're going to be the new mommy's main supporting cast member.
- Do NOT underestimate the value of a great babysitter. Treat them well!

- Always be gentle, but don't get paranoid that you will break them. Bumps and falls happen.
- Zippers are your ally. If the item of clothing doesn't have one, reconsider another outfit.
- Pick a favorite song for you both, and sing it to them often. It is a lasting connection.
- It's OK to just do things for the baby without asking for permission from your partner. You are a parent too, not just an assistant. Don't second guess yourself every five minutes.
- Establish eating and sleeping routines. We will only remind you of this another hundred times. Stick with it!
- Work cannot outweigh parenthood. Find the balance.
- Change those nappies!
- Inspect the poop. It might seem overbearing, but you are keeping tabs on the baby's health and wellbeing.

FILTER THROUGH IT. THE MISCONCEPTIONS

B ig steps are coming on the day your baby arrives and with it a world of information, advice, and all of the misconceptions that come with it. You won't know what to expect in so many aspects of parenting to start with. Like many of us, you may have heard a wealth of beliefs about babies or being a dad that simply are not true, or miss the mark.

This chapter addresses common false beliefs and myths, from your ability as a father and your child's future behaviors to financial preparation and buying products. Let's weed out those myths and the misguidance about parenting and child-rearing.

GAME CHANGER - THINKING THINGS WILL GO BACK TO NORMAL

Contrary to the changes you expect or hope will come with a new life, at some point, your subconscious may start to wonder when things will go back to normal. They won't. After the initial shock of the first few months or even years, you won't want them to, either.

You will learn so many new things and realize even more as a parent. Take all of it in stride as a new addition to your life. To complement this, debunking misconceptions will help you have a better idea of how your new normal as a dad should look.

MOM VS. DAD - FALLACIES ABOUT FATHERHOOD

Moms are better at parenting- There tends to be a common belief that motherly instincts are superior to those of the father. While it is true that "no one loves you like your mother," the same goes for dads in their very own way. Paternal responsibility and accountability are just as inherent in dads as parenting abilities are in moms. Don't buy into the idea that you are less adequate or necessary to your child, or that you are not built to be a good parent. We all have the capacity to be great parents and to learn how to be better parents.

Moms come first - One very harmful and frequent occurrence during pregnancy is for only the mother to receive attention and care. While she is carrying the baby and must have both of their needs met and seen to, ignoring the father's needs is very detrimental. Whether you ignore your own needs and feelings, or those around your family for the duration of the pregnancy neglect you, not addressing yourself as important to the event is a big mistake. Take good care of yourself and make sure you acknowledge the importance of your role to the success of bringing your child into the world. Don't throw a fit for attention, but speak up if you are struggling with feeling left out or pushed aside.

Dads know less - Another misnomer suggests that dads are not as clued in to the needs of their children, or don't know as much about taking care of babies. As mentioned above, anyone can gain the experience to meet their child's needs. Spending time with your little one will invest you with all of the knowledge you need about them. As you set their routine and learn their individual habits, you will get to know how to best tend to your baby like no one else ever could. We will talk more about learning and teaching yourself the skills you need in the next chapter.

Men want children less - Earlier in their lives, some men may seem less inclined to desire a family due to cost or perceived freedoms, but sooner or later, men want children as much as women. In polls taken several years ago in the US, as many as 8 in 10 men want to be dads one day, compared to only 7/10 of women (Villines, 2015). Safe to say, you may already feel how untrue this myth is in your own desires to have children.

Dad is less needed - There is a perception that mothers are the most necessary presence for every infant, to the exclusion of the father. Don't be fooled, your presence is just as important to your child's development and health as their mother's. In addition to your own invaluable contribution to your baby, you act as the other half of the time needed for caring in team parenting. Mom needs breaks and there is no such thing as giving your baby too much attention. Each parent has irreplaceable caring to give that will only promote your child's health and well-being.

Dads are too rough - Whether from a sense of adventure or the misconception of men being tougher, dads are very often viewed as the rougher parent, or 'too rough' with children. This comes, in part, from many fathers' desire to engage in adventurous fun with their children, or wanting to teach them the value of risk and danger and how to avoid and navigate it. The misconception here is that only dads do this. Wrestling and rough housing aren't exclusive to either parent and in just as many cases it applies to neither parent. You may hear other myths around this line of criticism about various problems that can come to your baby from 'rougher' treatment. One example of this is that bouncing babies on your knee can make them bow-legged or that getting them active and sitting up too soon can cause back problems. This, much like the lie that holding your baby too much will spoil them, is simply untrue.

STAYING POWER - "IT'S BETTER TO GO STRAIGHT HOME AFTER THE BIRTH."

When the day of the delivery comes, you will be in a mad dash to get to the hospital, settle in and wait for the birth to begin. The next logical step will seem to be to take your new baby right home. This is a common desire, to get past the inherent stress of the hospital and a rush to get back to some sense of normalcy at home. However, you may be causing yourself unnecessary distress by doing so.

To begin with, you will be high-strung and tired. The mother of your child even more so. The last thing you need is to go right home and stay up all night with a crying newborn. Besides that, you may worry over every sound or unusual reaction your baby has at first.

You should reconsider and stay an extra night or two in the hospital. It can offer you several advantages and relieve a world of stress. Most importantly, the nurses at the hospital can be instrumental in helping you learn everything you need to know before you go home and offer you peace of mind.

There will be lots of tests that need to be run, cluster feedings, and a ton of other interruptions throughout the first night. By the second night, you will be glad to stay put and let the staff assist you.

When it comes to your options for your stay, consult your doctor and the hospital to see what selections and requests you can make. Deciding your course of action ahead of time is very important to the process so they can have everything ready for you. Rooming-in or a variation of it might be exactly what you never knew you needed.

Longevity - The benefits of rooming-in can extend to after you go home. Statistics show that having your baby in the same room for the first six months of life reduces the risk of SIDS by 50%. Breastfeeding will be much easier if you do not have to get up and go to another room. Breastfeeding on demand usually takes

CHAPTER 3 | 63

some getting used to and training the breasts to react when needed. The baby's immediate access can help this process progress more naturally (Weiss, 2021).

PURCHASING POWER - "BABIES NEED A LOT OF THINGS"

At first, it may feel as if there are far too many things that you think you absolutely need. You assume you must buy every product and gadget on the market to meet the needs of your baby. They wouldn't make the products if they weren't necessary or useful, right?

Then, as you start changing diapers and feeding and living your day-to-day life with your new baby, you will start to understand the things you actually can't live without, and most things you worried and fussed about, you barely use at all. Finding out ahead of time what you will actually use will save you a whole lot of time and money.

Try to whittle that list down to the bare necessities before you bring your baby home.

Junk - Most cheap-looking plastic toys and tools are just that, cheap. So many accessories are a waste of money and will likely break with the average wear and tear of constant use.

Don't get every bell and whistle. You need the basics first and can grow from there.

Stock up - the consumables should be at the top of the list. Food, diapers, baby bags, and anything else you will want multiples of to always have ready to go. Better to have those extra changes of clothes than all of those toys your infant won't play with for several months yet.

New accounts and bills - Babies come with a lot of extra expenses including additions to your health care accounts and insurance plans. You also may need to spend money on childcare all too soon.

Backup plans - If you don't already have one, purchase a life insurance policy. Have that security firmly in hand that your child will have something to fall back on for care if something happens to you

Goals - Now is not the time to buy a new house, even with your growing family. Put some of those long-term goals on hold until you fully have a handle on your new budget with your child factored in. Long-term financial planning is very wise, but the short term should take priority with an added mouth to feed and more than a handful of unknowns to come in the next few years.

Stability - All of this boils down to figuring out your new normal, financially and functionally. Implement and use a household budget to work in all of the costs of the baby(RL360, 2022).

In the grand scheme of things, multiple factors will define your financial success. Address the matters most relevant to your baby first. Then spend some time really analyzing your goals and reassessing your plans.

Try to touch on all of these subjects:

- Reassess every short and long-term financial goal to accommodate this new life in your life.
- You need more emergency savings and planning money. Aim to have 3-6 months of living expenses saved at all times.
- Consider a savings account for your child. Putting money aside for them to use is a great gift with forethought for their future. However, don't let it hurt your retirement or current living.
- Check out nurseries and childcare locales before your baby arrives. You do not want to have to rush and waste money where you could have found a cheaper or better sitter. Get on the waiting list for the place you really want.
- Automate your spending when you can. You won't remember to pay for things when you are consumed with your newborn. Keep in mind

that this works best for consistent bills that don't change every month.

- Start teaching your children about money management early on to give them a sense of how things work. You are teaching your child skills to live, so start them early in the way the family operates, they are a contributing member too.

- Try to plan memorable events. Vacations, birthday parties. You want them to have fond memories of their childhood. Remember, it doesn't have to be outrageous, just things they will enjoy like stay-cations, family movie nights at the theater, etc.

GROWING PAINS - UNDERESTIMATING YOUR CHILD'S ACCELERATION

Most new parents majorly underestimate how fast their child accelerates. Kids grow unbelievably quickly and gain new skills just as quickly. That means they will be moving fast before long and you will have to keep up.

Unfortunately, babies do not develop a sense of danger to go along with their fast movement. Do not learn this lesson the hard way; it's your responsibility to keep them safe and teach them the rules.

You need to be prepared with the means to accommodate their growth and their mobility as soon as possible. Undoubtedly you will underestimate some clothing sizes, but you must anticipate their increased movement and physical capabilities. Children love to run and play. Your baby is heading for that milestone soon.

Use techniques to keep them in sight and controlled as they learn to control themselves:

- Stay close to them at all times. They will test this every now and then and see how it works and how you react to them, but never let them try it in a crowded area.
- Show them the safe places to run. You have to let them burn off energy, but you also have to be able to keep up.
- Lay down guidelines and parameters. This teaches self-control and rule-following skills.
- Keep them busy and entertained; bored kids get into trouble. Have them help you clean, and carry things. Give them a job so they not only feel included and occupied, they learn that these things are part of life and the family.
- Always keep a toy with you to distract and slow them down.

Finally, talk to them and give them clear expectations and that there are always consequences to their actions. Inform them how you want them to behave. As they grow, they will experiment with the boundaries, but be clear, consistent, and repeat what is expected of them. They must learn that they cannot always do what they want to do.

Don't leave it up to them at first, tell them the rules and make sure they follow them until they are capable of doing so on their own. Following up with the framework of punishments will help them develop the ability to discern how they choose to act around you as they become their own person.

Running away - They won't always run away from you. It is a phase. However, while they are in that phase, you can help by always using their stroller. In the stroller, you can keep them busy and distracted with toys and games so they don't feel like a prisoner. As they grow, implement the stroller as a punishment for breaking the rules when they are walking with you. The more independent they become, the worse of a punishment this will feel like.

One method to avoid negative words or punishment while they are in their running phase is to reverse the 'chasing' game to have them come after you. Diverting them from getting in the habit of running from you is a crucial training tool. You don't want to encourage the 'catch me' game. They may decide to play it at a very bad time in public (Gallie, 2014).

Carriers, harnesses, wrist straps - These can help to keep them close and contained if you want to allow them to move about near you. Be careful of the 'dog leash' mentality; for many kids, this acts as a trigger to misbehave when they are "let loose". At some point, you will need to introduce free movement if they are ever going to learn how to regulate themselves and understand their environment.

Returning home - Early on, you may get flustered or panic if your child runs away in public. If it makes you feel better, go home, but don't assume they will understand the connection of having to leave due to their actions.

Warnings - Toddlers do not understand the meaning of your "no" if you don't back it up with consequences. "No" has to mean *stop, stop now,* and you make them stop immediately. This is the only way to effectively teach them to obey in chaotic situations. Eventually, you can give them the chance to reconsider their actions, but they have to understand your reasoning to be able to do so.

Safety - Start your child early with safety learning tools. Read them safety stories and put those techniques into practice so they see the application of safety rules (Gallie, 2014).

BEING BETTER - "BECOMING A DAD MEANS BECOMING A BETTER PERSON"

A fallacy many fathers fall prey to is expecting to become a different person as soon as their baby is born. Ask your own parents sometimes how they felt when they had you. The invincible and all-knowing people you remember growing up were just like you are now.

Many of us have that illusion, envisioning our parents as having it together, running the show, and confidently managing our family's lives. If you ask them though, they were just figuring it all out like you are.

The reality of the situation is that becoming a parent doesn't automatically mean you become a better or even different person. Changing the things that will make you the best person and father you can be is entirely up to you. And you *can* do it!

There are a few things that are relatively easy to do that will guarantee that you achieve the parenting you set out to do even without knowing "how to parent" yet.

They are founded in core needs that will benefit your child:

- Confidence and self-esteem building. This can be nurtured through support, engagement, love, and affection.
- Spending time. This is a face-value concept. You cannot be a positive influence in your child's life if you aren't there to get to know them.
- Discipline. Rules and structure backed with positivity and consistency.
- Act out the behaviors and values you want your child to aspire to. Be the role model by establishing your authority as a source of valuable information and wisdom early on.
- Instruct your child. Teach them lessons, explain reasons and inform them about the way things are.
- Eat together. Bonding as a family over dinner is one of the best forums for learning about each other and making your child feel valued and understood. They will learn the value of caring about others through shared experiences and listening.
- Read to them. Reading is an intimate and developmental tool.

- Show respect to your child's other parent. No matter the family status, treat them with kindness. Seeing you accept and respect each other shows them how to do the same and to feel those same feelings of appreciation.
- Start early. Be there, and show them how much you want to be their parent (BHE Team, 2021).

OTHER URBAN MYTHS

There are more than a few old tales floating around about caring for your baby. Make sure you debunk any false information before trying them out on your child (McGuinness, 2022).

- Cereal helps your baby sleep. This misconception falls in line with the fact that your baby will generally start to sleep through the night about the same time they start eating stage 1 solid foods.
- Water, tea, or diluted milk for hydration. Babies don't need water yet, they only need breast milk or formula. Giving them other liquids can cause a sodium imbalance and be hazardous to their health.
- Drooling and putting things in their mouth is a sign of teething. This is not always the case. All

babies put things in their mouths at some point. It's a common stage of development.

- Belly sleeping is soothing or more comfortable for your baby. This is actually extremely dangerous for your baby. Despite old advice saying that it's good for them, belly sleeping is a leading cause of SIDS (Sudden Infant Death Syndrome). The best position for your baby to sleep in is on their back.
- Fevers and medicine. Not all illnesses need a quick fix. Keep your baby hydrated and monitor them closely if they have a fever but do not jump to conclusions. Sometimes it's simply a natural response to vaccines, ear infections, viruses, or other immune responses.
- Giving Tylenol before a vaccine to reduce pain. Studies show that this is not only ineffective against the pain of a shot, but the Tylenol can actually have an adverse effect on the effectiveness of the vaccine.
- Spoiling your baby by holding them too much. Babies need skin-to-skin contact to grow and be healthy. Never fear holding them too much. You don't always have to be holding them either, but holding them is the best way to assess their needs and form a deep bond.

- Single food introduction, or phasing in foods. Many parents try introducing one food at a time when they switch to solids and wait for their baby to adjust. This can actually cause nutritional imbalances. All stage 1 foods can be introduced at the same time without issue. (Allergies excepted) (McGuinness, 2022).

Takeaway Tips:

- Don't rush home. Stay the extra night in the hospital. The knowledge and health benefits will surprise you.
- Set boundaries with family members wanting to babysit, but also hold them to it when they want to! You need their help.
- Stick to the basics on buying baby gear and accessories.
- Focus on stability in your finances in the early years. Be cautious about big expenditures. Make a plan for the financial future of your child, including daycares, savings, and everyday necessities.
- Plan for runaway babies. Keep them in sight or on a close link to avoid losing them. Allow for some freedom to let them learn to stay close.

- You won't change overnight. You decide who you will be as a parent.
- Be careful where you get your baby advice from. Check the facts on hearsay and "classic" childcare techniques; people don't always know what they're talking about.

4

KNOW YOUR ROLE, DO YOUR PART!

N ew fathers often fail to be proactive in their newfound responsibilities, leading to common mistakes and problems that could be avoided with a little research. Your role as a father is not a cut-and-dry list of specific duties, but you have to do your part to learn what you can offer. Part of that will include defining what your role will encompass and fulfilling those expectations.

Every day you will feel the pressure to perform, and more so once your child is part of the picture. You may even feel overwhelmed with the many tasks that you have to do and not feel equipped to handle them. However, refusing to prepare is a huge mistake that many parents make.

To that end, you must learn how to expand your capabilities. Incorporating a better mentality and systems, as well as greater knowledge of your new job will elevate you to the task and prepare you to come through for your child and partner. The only way we can be better fathers is through hard work. This involves being proactive in preparation, practice, working closely with your partner, and research.

LEARNING TO LEARN - NOT TAKING THE TIME TO LEARN

Something we are rarely taught how to do is to teach ourselves, or how to research new topics properly. The study skills, the discipline, and the vast range of abilities that enable us to learn are essential parts of being a better dad. This is why you are reading this book, but in order to retain and use this information, you need the translational skills to make good advice a reality in your life.

Research skills can help you understand not only how to find the information you need, but how to use it, when to use it, and how to pass it on to your family. The benefits span from helping your child with homework to legal paperwork and simply finding the best options in purchases for your family and child.

'**Funneling**' - Start big and work your way down to small. This is a great technique to use when trying to learn something new by starting with broad or general subject matter and working your way into the detailed and more complex. Much like fixing a car, you don't just start taking things apart without understanding how they function or work together with the other parts. You have to have a basic understanding of a topic to grow on. Google is not a bad place to just throw out your question, to begin with, but you need to expand your resources to answer the harder questions. Once you have a solid foundation, you can focus your learning on the finer details of a subject.

Reliable sources - You also must be able to recognize whether where you are getting the information is a valid or reputable source. This involves critical thinking and asking the right questions about the source of the material. Is it well researched, and does it have comparable sources that line up with the message and information? Is there a conflict of interest in the content or regarding the writer's motives?

Verify - Whenever possible, try to verify the information you are getting. The internet is a free and open forum to say anything and everything. This puts information at risk from twists to skewed opinions or outright lies. Cross-checking with a few sources can help to get a better picture of the truth of the source, or just how fluid the topic really is. How many sides of the argument are there?

Keep an open mind - Be open to answers you didn't expect or that differ from what you believe. It is possible you have been wrong. Another skill that goes into wisdom and intelligence is learning how to accept when we are wrong and modifying our beliefs to accommodate new information. It sounds silly, but in order to learn, you have to be open to learning.

Staying organized - Organization is very important when you research. Take notes, document your study, and write down where you got the information from. You won't need to cite your sources in everyday life, but it is good to know where you found them to pass along when you share your knowledge with others.

Libraries - Libraries are still a very useful source of learning. Most cities have one. Use them to learn things you need to know and even better, want to know. Especially with parenting. They have books on just about every subject. Their learning resource staff are also a great way to get the help you need and they will teach you how to find what you're looking for.

Using study skills and research can be applied to debunking myths, a new toy for your baby, knowing how to handle worrisome situations with childhood illness, or helping them to learn about volcanoes for school projects. You are their go-to source of teaching, so learn how to find source material to provide them with (MasterClass staff, 2021).

Intellectual growth will change the way you think and have positive effects on your fatherhood as well as many other areas of your life.

ASK AWAY - TRYING TO DO IT ALL YOURSELF WITHOUT ASKING FOR HELP

Over the next couple of decades, you will constantly be learning new things about how to be a parent. One of the most integral resources you must not forget, or refuse to use, is asking for help.

Trying to do it all on your own is an amateur mistake. A lot like pretending that everything is alright and fine when you know deep down that everything is NOT OK. Stay alert for signs of depression.

- Fatigue or chronic exhaustion.
- Moodiness, or struggling to regulate your emotions.
- Lack of appetite, or overeating for comfort.
- Overwhelming sadness or despair.

- Inability to perform basic tasks and self-care, apathy.

Ask your friends and family and they will likely be more than glad to help you in any way they can. Never assume that anyone knows what's going on inside your head and are simply unwilling to volunteer. They have lives of their own and may not know you are struggling. Especially if you tell them you are fine when they do ask. Be honest.

Observation can act as a tool for instructing us as fathers. You have experiences seeing your dad, or friends' dads and how they handled things with you as a child or with their babies. Some of your friends may have already gone through first-time-dad trials. These are the people who can give you advice, and a helping hand, when you come to them.

Be humble in asking for assistance. If they have more experience than you, you need what they have to offer. Pride does not serve your baby in any way, and bravado will end with you still missing the skills you need and you looking foolish on top of it all.

You have a variety of resources at your disposal:

- Make a list of useful references, and helpers, and even write down the advice they give you.

- Consult with a mentor, dad, or father figure.
- Talk with fellow dads ahead of you or going through the same things.
- Seek out help from literature.
- Look up info online or find blogs and support groups like 'New Dads United!' on Facebook to ask about things you need to know.

Many of us are taught from an early age, whether culturally, or by our family and peers, to be independent and pull ourselves up. A pervasive mentality has poisoned a lot of people into believing that expressing emotions or admitting their failures is a sign of weakness.

Now that does not mean you do not need to know how to take care of yourself or self-regulate your emotions. It does mean that you might need to relearn some things and seek assistance changing your behaviors. Sometimes it's as simple as having a friend to be there while you apply what you already know, to work through the hurdles keeping you from proceeding.

PROFESSIONAL HELP

In addition to asking for help, there may come a time when seeking professional solutions are necessary. Mental and emotional distress need specialized attention. No one questions when you take your car into the shop for a mechanic's appraisal or when you call your attorney about a legal matter. We need to apply the same logic to our well-being. Consulting an expert should be a given.

Unfortunately, too many people don't, or won't. According to data from the Health Insurance Fund of Australia, only 1 in 5 people with psychological illnesses or related issues seek help for their malady (Happy, 2019).

While a spotlight has been shined on many medical problems and general ignorance about physical health is on the decline, psychological ailments have a long way to go. For example, the tests for postpartum depression in women have not been modified for assessing dads yet (Peate, 2020). It's up to you to talk to someone, be it your doctor or a friend, and find the root of the problem before it harms you and subsequently, your baby.

Be strong enough to know when you are not feeling your best and ask for the help you need. Your child and partner will thank you for it and be there to support your decision and your recovery.

BACKSEAT PARENTING - NOT STAYING INVOLVED

Your child is part of you, or rather, you are part of them. No matter how involved or not, you will see some of your behavior in their development. Forming those developments relies on your involvement in guiding the things you contributed to your child genetically.

The more time and effort you put in, the better your family will be for the hard work. Sitting back and watching events unfold is too easy when we feel over-whelmed, but you have a responsibility and a role to play.

- You are learning all of the tools you will need to get the job done.
- You must keep a close watch on yourself to keep from slacking off or letting go.

Mom cannot do this job alone, and should not have to when the other parent is willing to participate. Too many single parents manage alone, to the detriment of the child and parent. It's also your duty to watch your child's mother for signs of this. If you are alert and stay on top of it, neglect will not get the better of you (Welch, 2012).

THE LITTLE THINGS - MINOR MISHAPS

Now it's time to address mistakes on a much smaller scale. These are work-related, clumsy, or minor inconveniences, but often just as problematic to your everyday progress in parenthood, and they follow right along with learning and teaching yourself and your child.

Children don't always understand the seriousness of some things like important paperwork and why they shouldn't draw on it or your work computer with markers and why they shouldn't drink juice in dad's office.

On the other hand, you don't always remember to lock the door, put the items away or notice when they are playing with your work phone until it's too late.

SCREEN TIME - NOT PROTECTING YOUR DEVICES FROM YOUR BABY

In this technological era, devices will be a part of your baby's life from the very start. You may even get them a tablet to watch cartoons and play educational games in the car or during long waits for the doctor's office. Technology can be a very useful tool for occupying your baby.

It can also be a small-scale disaster if you don't take precautions.

When it comes to your phone, your baby will be equally fascinated with it as they are with any glowing, pretty device or toy. They may even be more interested in your phone because of how important they see that it is to you. And they will not understand the difference between their devices and your devices, at least until they are a little older.

Despite this lack of awareness of whose toy is whose, they certainly have all of the skills needed to open things you don't want them getting into and deleting important work emails or documents that you need. Or they might just like the worst sort of tweets and Instagram posts by accident (Herrick, 2019).

If you don't have a designated device for your baby, be very careful that they stay in the app you allow them to play. Deleting apps is another extremely fun activity for little ones.

Fortunately, there are a bunch of solutions to help you prevent these mishaps and still be able to use your phone as a distraction when needed. Most device companies and operating systems offer an array of filters, guided browsing, and permissions that can be set up to prevent this sort of unwanted activity from happening. Even if they get a hold of your phone without your permission.

Tools to use:

- Options like 'guided access' in Apple devices and restriction passwords are a great way of limiting access to your little ones on your device.
- Android offers a pin function that does not allow your child to exit an app without your unlock code.
- Two-step security is a feature you can program on most purchasing apps. You can also change your payment settings to require a password entry before purchase to avoid in-game expenditures or google/apple store app purchases by your child, intentional or not.
- Add another limited profile to your device. You can program it with only the apps you want them to use.

Much like parental controls on your TV and streaming services, you need to be able to monitor what your little one is doing, at first simply for preventing silly mistakes, but later to prevent them from exploring things that might be harmful, or that you would prefer they not be exposed to.

If you prefer a service for the task, there are some paid services for both your computer and phone that can manage your child's experience on a device. The cost may seem rather silly at first, but it is well worth the peace of mind to know they are safe and so are your irreplaceable photos and documents.

Lastly, backup your devices! With everything invested in our technology nowadays, it's too easy to lose precious memories when they are only in one location that could crash or malfunction.

GEARING UP - RESEARCHING YOUR PURCHASES

There is too much gear out there. Plain and simple. You can't and shouldn't buy it all. And certainly not without reviewing or trying out the product first. Popular brands of course receive the most reviews and the most attention. This can be deceiving. Use your new study skills to sift through the good and the bad and get what is best for you. Below are some useful tips for buying gear:

- Consult other parents. Find out what breaks, and what lasts. They can also help you cut down on what you don't actually need. They may also know of products you have never heard of that can make your life easier. A fun example is 'light-switch extenders' for toddlers to be able to turn on lights.

- Think about what you will be using the product for. Will it meet all of your needs?
- Be careful not to buy things that won't fit in your house or car.
- Ask employees at the store. Often they have a pretty good idea of what items get returned, which are most purchased, and so on.

Shopping online is a modern marvel that we all benefit from. There is nothing wrong with ordering what you need and having it delivered, but consider going to a store to explore some options before you do. Trying it in person is the only way to see how a stroller drives, a carrier carries, and how heavy certain items like car seats are in person.

Watch and Learn - Many brands advertise their ease of 'pack and play' or similar ideas, but are not as easy as they show. Watch videos of other parents using products before settling on the ones you plan to buy.

Compare and Contrast - When you go to browse, take your partner with you. You are built differently, and one of you might be using a certain item more than the other. Make decisions as a family.

Peer Review - Reading reviews can often not give an accurate portrayal. Some comments are opinions, or in some cases, are simply not true (Domestikated Life, 2017).

The last line of review comes from your baby. Some items will have to get the baby's stamp of approval when you try them out on your child and they either take to it or don't.

BEDTIME STORIES - LETTING MOM DO ALL THE READING

One error that seems to be a common trend in parenting is mothers doing the majority, if not all of the reading to children. Some of this may come from cultural leanings or typically accepted norms, or just from negligence on the part of dads. Not everyone is interested in reading, but reading to your kids is extremely beneficial to you both.

Reading to your children promotes an appreciation for learning and encourages brain development. Especially if both parents do it. Don't miss out on the meaningful aspects of your relationship that reading can develop between you and your child.

Language development - It is a well-established fact that reading to children is critical to their literacy and language development, but only recently have there been any studies done exclusively on the effects of fathers reading to their kids and how it increases their overall learning capabilities.

A study led by Dr. Quach of the Murdoch Children's Research Institute and Melbourne University (Early Learning, 2018), showed that both parents' influence through reading had a significant impact on the enhancement of literary competence in children. These results held true regardless of the income, or education levels of the parents. Results also indicated that children who had fathers who read to them in addition to their mothers had even higher scores and that there was a direct correlation between being read to by Dad and language development. This was greater than literacy in the children observed.

In other words, the more both parents read to their children, the better those kids performed across the board.

The study attributed this to several different factors:

- Different ways various people read aloud.
- How captivated the audience is and how that audience interprets the reading.
- Emphasis and pronunciation variations.

The main factor that was noted in improved development was how more fathers tended to break the reading down into small, bite-sized sections to ensure that the child understood the material before moving on. In cases where mothers did the same, the results were similar.

The takeaway is clear. Read to your child. Be the bookworm that inspires your young one to learn and grow. It's an excellent way to bond and cultivate similar interests within your family (Early Learning, 2018). And who doesn't like a good story? Act it out, get fun and silly, and your kids will love it.

Especially a story with a happy ending!

Takeaway Tips:

- Take time to build your skill sets to be the best father you can be. This means learning to learn better and how to put what you learn into practice.
- Ask for advice from others who have experience with dad issues.
- Use device protection software like profiles, app screen locks, or child protection service apps to guide your baby's use of your device. If you can afford it, buy a device for your baby to watch things on that is theirs.

- Always make copies and backup your data.
- Don't let yourself get overwhelmed alone. Communicate with a friend or family.
- Research or ask around about baby products. Someone's tried it and can guide you.
- Read the reviews, but try out the item in the store if you can. In the end, less is more. If you aren't sure, don't buy it.
- Read to your children from an early age. It's fun and instrumental to their development.

5

KEEP YOUR HEAD IN THE GAME, PSYCHOLOGICAL AND EMOTIONAL STRUGGLES

Aside from the physical strains of exhaustion, the most taxing and draining aspect of parenthood will be emotional and psychological pressure. Some days will feel insurmountable, even with only the bare minimum to accomplish, however, they won't dominate your life or your relationship with your child. The mistakes that stem from our tired states usually manifest themselves in the form of carelessness and faltering attention to details. Forgetfulness, feeling inadequate, and lacking a sense of connection can cause a wide array of consequences ranging from overreacting, being too harsh in our discipline, to becoming overbearing or compensating to win our children's affections.

Keep a firm grasp on what kind of parent you want to be as you read about some of the most common careless failures that stand in the way of every potential parent. Staying alert and on top of the matter will help you curb the urge to let things slip by.

PARENTAL BLISS? - NOT FEELING THE 'MAGIC'

You might panic when they place your infant in your arms for the first time and you don't 'click' with your baby. Don't worry that something is wrong just because you don't feel magically entranced by your newborn.

Your child is a new person, and you have just been through a lot of stress to meet them. It is normal to feel nerves, unease, and a storm of emotions that will distract you from enjoying the first touch of your baby.

Relax and just be in the moment. You will look back and realize how much you really were just starting out with each tiny bonding moment from the very beginning (Welch, 2012).

GOOD ENOUGH - COMPARING YOUR KIDS

Inevitably, your child will be around other children, your friends will have kids and you will compare notes on when they did what. It's normal to match our growing little ones to the statistics and milestones. The danger arises when we start to get competitive and overly conscious when they don't all line-up.

The most important thing to remember about your child is that all babies develop at their own pace. Many of the traditional and textbook markers will follow suit. Your child might hit them all. Or none of them. Love your child and their progress for what it is. This is their journey. Putting unnecessary pressure on yourself or them does no one any good.

Measuring Up- The most common comparisons tend to be height and weight milestones among parents. In many cases, it starts to become more about competing with other parents than anything else. Secondarily, other aspects like learning curves and motor skill development will stand out as achievements. They are to be celebrated, but not held up against other children's progress (Shapin, 2019).

More often than not, you and other parents will base your commentary on perception, hearsay, and opinion. These conversations will get in your head, making you doubt your baby's health, normality, and your parenting ability

Identity - Your baby is the center of your life, so you will take so many things personally about them. Once again, this is perfectly natural. We all compare ourselves to others regularly in many ways. What you must try to avoid is projecting this comparative culture onto your child. Do not let your insecurities define who they are (Shapin, 2019).

From pregnancy to the time they move out of the house, you will find things to second guess over, wondering if you were up to standard as a parent. Only compare yourself to yourself from yesterday. Don't let this type of analysis stick or you will be doing it the rest of their lives.

No one is like you. No one is like your child or their mother.

When you feel unsure, remind yourself that percentiles, milestones, and brackets are designed for generalizations, to describe or categorize for medical averages. The actual ranges for when a baby might start eating solid foods, start teething, or walking vary so drastically despite the statistical averages.

Set your own milestones and don't get caught up on the web fussing over expectations. Trust your own knowledge of your child and if someone starts a conversation comparing kids, just step away, or change the subject.

The most fulfilling thing you can do is enjoy your baby's journey through their growth without a critical eye.

THE FUN ONE - TRYING TO BUY YOUR CHILDREN'S AFFECTION

Neither parent should be labeled as a singular role, or you are not both parenting. If one of you is 'fun' and the other the serious or disciplinarian most of the time, something is wrong. As a team, you and your partner need balance and even distribution of responsibilities.

Favorites - Everyone wants to be their kid's favorite person, but you have to understand that you probably will be for most of their lives, and then at some point, you may not be. A sure-fire way to wind up falling out of favor is to fail to be a parent. This may seem counter-intuitive, but more people appreciate their parents for actually doing their job later in life.

On the other hand, trying to buy their affection for your own satisfaction is selfish and harmful to your relationship with your child and with your partner. Bribing your child skews their perspective of your role in their life, and the other parent who might refuse to give them treats constantly. The imbalance and inconsistency of rewards is very confusing to children and creates resentment against discipline.

The fact of the matter is that you cannot always have a good time in life. You recognize this at work and other responsibilities, and the same applies to parenthood. Sharing the burden, and sharing the joy with your partner will foster stability and contentment. Don't deprive your partner of the good times for your own sake.

When you feel drawn to play the fun parent, remember that your children might not take you seriously if there is such an uneven footing in the home. Teetering between rules and no rules is exhausting for kids.

Often, this type of behavior results in resentment between partners, and in cases of marriage, divorce, and dissolution of the family unit. Not all home environments are the same or have to be, but more often than not, events that separate the family or drastically change the dynamic and structure of life are very damaging and traumatic to children

Someone will always have to be the parent. If you are not fulfilling that side of your role, then you are the problem and your partner will suffer for it.

Three typical outcomes tend to mark the end of this type of parenting when addressed:

- Kids will get bored with the fake behavior and not want a part of it, the parent guilty of buying favor will stop because their perceived role is gone.
- Occasionally, the parent realizes their error and goes back to being a 'normal' parent.
- The third option is that they stop being a parent altogether and disappear from their child's life.

Ultimately, your children will respect you for bringing stability to their lives and for being present. And if they don't you know that you at least did your best.

To alleviate feeling like a stern and authoritarian parent, try:

- Doing kind things for yourself and your partner that make you feel fun and silly without compromising your role.
- Engage in fun family activities where everyone has the chance to unwind and laugh.
- Talk to your partner and divide up the duties, chores, punishments, and rewards. Both parents should be known for all of the above.
- Practice self-care and finding contentment. Your children will see your pleasant nature and your efforts to do better for them.

"DON'T CRY!" - STOPPING YOUR CHILD'S TEARS

Whether it's because of culture, or preference, or just getting irritated, you might try to make your child stop crying. Ask them, tell them, insist that they hide their tears. It must be made clear that this is emotional suppression and it is not healthy.

Children need to cry. Frankly, so do you. And you need to show them it is OK to express their emotions when they need to. Besides, telling them to stop does not work. And when they fail you and you get mad because they can't comply, they feel even worse and can develop a complex.

Processing - Letting them cry allows them to learn how to sort through their feelings. Children, especially very little ones, use crying to express their limited methods of dealing with powerful feelings.

Teaching - If you shut down every tearful encounter, you also limit the number of teachable moments. You can instruct them how to use and manage their emotions and how to self-soothe.

If you are tempted, remember when you have been told to stop whining or crying growing up, or in your adult life. We all have experienced the shame that comes with those comments.

Instead, try:

- Comfort item with a toy or comfort item for them to focus their sadness or frustration on.
- Hug them. Let hugs do what they are meant for.
- Place a hand on their back, let them know it's all right and that you're there for them.
- Give them space. You need it when you are going through something. Time and space do wonders for healing (Garcia, 2021).

The simple rule is, don't tell your child to stop crying. Restricting childrens' emotions can have long-lasting effects on their development and adjustment to the world. It can send the message to your child that you only like them when they are happy.

CONSEQUENCES - NOT TEACHING YOUR CHILD ABOUT CAUSE AND EFFECT

Stress and fear can make us do some pretty ridiculous things. None of us can bear to witness our children in pain. Every instinct in you as a parent demands you to stop any harm from coming to them. Nonetheless, life is full of cause and effect, actions and consequences.

You cannot protect your child from learning lessons from their behavior and actions.

Sometimes you have to allow your child to fail. Sooner or later it is unavoidable and they need to slowly grow into understanding how to handle those trials on their own. Preventing lesson learning and suffering consequences can have even worse outcomes. Your child can't be prepared to keep themselves safe if you never let them practice using those skills.

Children who have overprotective parents often show signs of anxiety and depression. This can stem from unreasonable demands of perfection or from having no control over any facet of their own life (ChoosingTherapy.com, 2022).

HOVERING - BEING OVERPROTECTIVE

Generally, overprotective parenting comes from insecurities in the parent and low self-esteem that is projected onto the child. The statistics show that it is a very common issue (ChoosingTherapy.com, 2022).

62% of parents report that they are sometimes overprotective. Half of most parents want to be more involved in their child's life and decisions and should be more involved in their child's education. 85% of parents talk frequently to their child's teacher about their progress

(ChoosingTherapy.com, 2022). That in and of itself is not a bad thing, but too often parents intervene on behalf of their child in compliance with authoritative measures.

Signs of overprotective parenting:

- Taking over projects and tasks (especially school for a good grade).
- Continuous oversight of all of a child's activities, checking in constantly when apart.
- Controlling child's friendships.
- Excessive anger warnings, preventing age-appropriate risks.
- Overbearing, doing all chores and waiting on the child, over-dependency.
- Planning all activities and life of the child, social control.

(ChoosingTherapy.com, 2022)

If you are prone to this sort of behavior, look into ways you can work through it. Therapy can help immensely, in group sessions or individual counseling. Between you and your child, seek the intervention of a third party to help you establish boundaries and mediate your interaction.

STERN WARNINGS - OVER-DISCIPLINING

When it comes to discipline in your home, finding the balance between tyrant and free-for-all can be a struggle. Your children need structure, but you don't want them to fear you.

We have touched on positive reinforcement in other areas of parenting. Try to use the same gentle hand here. Yelling and dealing severe punishments generally create resentment.

Our stress and irritation manifest in our discipline. We want to crack down on their grades, chores, or too much time spent with friends when we feel like they are influencing their performance negatively. Things would be so much easier if they would fall in line.

Sadly, this type of parenting comes with harsh consequences for your relationship with your kids.

In a study of students and faculty in Cambodia at the Royal University of Phnom Penh, many stated that they had no emotional connection with disciplinarian parents. In extreme situations, they witnessed threats and violence as punishment for disobedience. Most of these subjects suffered from stress-related insomnia, low self-esteem, depression, and anxiety (Vann, 2017).

Trauma almost always leads to trauma, so try to think about what you went through and if you are putting your child through the same things. They will judge themselves as you judge them, so be conscientious of what you say and how you say it. Break the cycle.

Try to implement kind language, positive enforcement, and reasonable approaches to your child-rearing (Shaw, 2019).

Positive reinforcement - Remind your child of how good behavior is better and can earn them rewards.

When they act out - Use terms like "I liked it when you...," and "I am happy when you..." They will respond so much more actively to pleasing and helping you than a simple encouragement or compliments about how good they are. You know how good it feels when someone acknowledges your helpful assistance (Gallie, 2014).

Takeaway Tips:

- Make a plan to be the best parent you can be. Think ahead so you don't make rash judgment calls.
- Your relationship with your baby will develop. Don't stress if you do not immediately feel a connection with your infant.

- Don't get sucked into comparisons with other people's kids. Yours is your own, and they are who they are. Let it be and enjoy it!
- Don't sit back and watch your partner raise your child. Stay involved and do not get complacent in your parenting.
- Check yourself to make sure you aren't playing the Disney Dad and pandering to instant gratification.
- Let your baby and your child cry. Show them it is OK to show and express emotions.
- You cannot prevent anything bad from ever happening to your child. Teach them how to be safe.
- Respect your child as a person and give them the courtesies you would expect.
- We all have scars, try not to give your kids the same hurts you received. Use kind words and foster a caring environment where they can approach you with their problems.

DANGER ZONE

Most of the mistakes that you will make with your child are ultimately nominal. Everything covered so far may keep you up at night, criticizing yourself for not quite getting it perfect. Eventually, you will find that the majority of that type of thinking is silly and that most of your little discrepancies will have little effect on your growing child as long as you are constantly updating your parenting style and correcting those mistakes when they happen.

There are, as we all have likely witnessed, matters of the home and parental shortcomings that lead to severe, traumatic experiences for children. The mistakes in this chapter are far less common but need to be addressed to stay aware of harmful situations that could befall your child.

All of the statistics and cautions are here to warn you, not to scare you. Take these matters to heart and do not let your child become a victim of neglect. Ignorance is not bliss in the case of risky scenarios for your children, but however extreme this might seem, raising awareness easily eliminates any chance of fatal or traumatic harm from affecting your family.

NEGLECTING YOUR CHILD

No one likes a backseat driver. But worse than that is when you need someone to navigate or give you directions and they remain silent. This analogy works well for neglectful or self-sidelined parents.

Neglect can appear in various forms, from ignoring physical needs to not giving emotional attention. Essentially, where parenting is concerned, it is the failure to respond to the needs of your child (Holland, 2021).

Neglectfulness is a common mistake that spiderwebs into all facets of your life. Where your role in your baby's life is concerned, attentive parenting should be near or at the top of your priorities with your child.

Effects of Negligence

According to the CDC (2022), 1 in 7 kids experienced abuse in some form in the United States in 2020. This includes neglect by parents or caretakers. This form of maltreatment is the most common form of abuse (American SPCC, 2022). The effects on the child in such circumstances are much more than just emotion. Physical, mental, and developmental problems stem from neglect and alter a young person's life into adulthood.

Physical Detriments of Neglect - Children who have lived through some sort of adverse situation during their early years are far more likely to suffer from physical ailments or developmental impairment. This is commonly a result of toxic stress during formative periods. The damage is mostly attributed to stunting of brain growth and development (Child Welfare Information Gateway, 2019).

Most commonly, the effects will not be immediately evident. Children suffering neglect or maltreatment have been shown to exhibit greater risks of later life health issues and long-term diseases. Diabetes, malnutrition, high blood pressure, and lung disease are far more common in children and subsequently adults who were subjected to childhood maltreatment, amongst other illnesses (Child Welfare Information Gateway, 2019).

In many cases, this damage extends backward to prenatal neglect and a failure to properly nourish or provide prenatal care during pregnancy which leads to birth complications. Most commonly, the culprit in the offending parent is substance abuse.

Other consequences of neglect on children include:

- Harmful effects on growth.
- Long-term illnesses and later life diseases.
- Diminished brain structure.

In more direct cases of harm from neglect, parents might ignore complaints of pain or discomfort from their child, which could develop into more serious ailments. Not addressing an infection such as ears, nose, or throat, for example, could lead to permanent damage when not tended to. Take your children's discomforts seriously and see a doctor before the problems get worse.

Fortunately, research has shown that children's brains can recover with proper intervention. However, the most effective method of addressing the issue is to prevent it altogether.

Non-organic Failures - Often, victims of neglect will show inexplicable symptoms and ailments that cannot be traced to an organ defect or definitive cause. These are called 'non-organic failures' in the cases of call children under the age of five. Most children with this issue tend to be drastically underweight, and generally underdeveloped.

It is important to note that in many cases there are underlying causes for unexplained poor development. Non-organic failures can be tied to psychological and social traumas as well as physical misdiagnosis such as a failure to identify chromosomal abnormalities, failure to note caloric wasting (persistent vomiting and losing nutrients), and miscalculating the food needs of the baby's growth rate (Venkateshwar et al, 2017).

Symptoms to look out for:

- Anemia.
- Dry, cracked skin.
- Iron deficiency.
- Slow or abnormal weight gain, or a drop in weight gain ratio
- (Venkateshwar et al, 2017).

Cognitive Detriments of Neglect - Children's mental health is made up of their social, emotional, and intellectual capacities. This includes all of their early attachments, their personality development, and social communication functions. Neglect has a negative effect on all of the above.

Children exposed to environments where they are starved for attention, nutrition, affection, and learning will form strange attachments to their caregivers and struggle to form any meaningful relationships with others. Victims of neglect are often known for being isolated and shut off. They can also be highly dependent on the source of their maltreatment. Often this leads to antisocial behaviors that can make them unable to cope with common situations and act out against social systems Child Welfare Information Gateway, 2019).

In cases of substance abuse on the part of the parent, the needs of the child are not met because of the parent's needs and desires for drugs. The child may exhibit signs in their behavior such as:

- Insecure relationship practices.
- Lack of emotional regulation.
- Failure to understand emotional expressions.
- Failure to differentiate between emotions.

- Easy to frustration and anger.

Academically, victims will struggle, as well. In many studies, scans displayed visible signs of diminished cerebral mass (Child Welfare Information Gateway, 2019). Psychological conditions may develop like attention deficits, frequently giving up, heightened stress levels, and 'zoning out'. It is your responsibility to address the negative impacts of childhood neglect for your child's future in adulthood.

The outcome of neglect is not something you would never wish on your child. Be attentive and prevent this abuse from entering your home. Neglecting your child can result in motor, language, and physical milestones all being hindered. These traumatic experiences alter the brain and can lead to later-life psychological conditions.

Parental Lows - Neglecting Each Other's Wellbeing

Being attentive to your child also means keeping a close eye on yourself and your partner. The reason you may feel less inclined to address your child's needs could have to do with your state of mind and emotions. Feeling sluggish or apathetic might just be a sign of exhaustion, but often it can indicate that you are suffering from a chemical imbalance that can cause depression and anxiety.

Both parents, and frankly all parents, are susceptible to depression, and studies show that while 10-15% of new mothers suffer from postpartum depression, 10-25% of dads are affected by it (Welch, 2012). Many experts believe this number is even higher than what is reported. This can be much more severe than the 'baby blues' you hear about. Look for signs of anxiety like irritability, racing thoughts, and uncontrollable mood swings.

Make sure you are getting sufficient:

- Exercise.
- Sleep (as much as you can manage with your baby).
- Eating well and enough.
- Discuss your symptoms openly and honestly with your doctor.

After all of the dangers and concerns regarding neglect we have covered so far, we must also address some of the most horrible mistakes you can make concerning your baby. This isn't to make you panic or scare you, but it is a reminder for you that all of us make mistakes, but where your baby is concerned, some mistakes can be fatal. Use this less as a warning but as an encouragement to be alert, responsible, and extra protective of your newborn.

DROWNING - DANGERS FOR BABIES IN WATER

Many of the terrible losses experienced by parents start with the phrase "I only turned my back for a second." It's not neglect, as much as distraction. Children can be reckless as we have touched on in previous chapters. They don't have a sense of danger or a fear of threats and you have to stay alert around potential hazards.

Especially in scenarios that are typically associated with fun for your little one. Like water. The fact of the matter is, that anyone can drown, but children are especially at risk. A leading cause of death in children ages 1-4 is drowning (Centers for Disease Control, 2022).

Your baby will come in contact with water sooner or later outside of bath time, whether it's for fun in the backyard during the summer or swimming activities at a pool or lake. Teaching your child to swim and to enjoy the water is one of the most enjoyable and happy experiences for both of you.

As long as you take every precaution, stay alert, and teach them the rules and safety measures along the way.

Water Level - It does not take a lot of water to put an infant in danger. Under a year old, the most common location for drowning is in the bathtub, accounting for 2/3 of the unfortunate accidents (Centers for Disease Control, 2022).

For this reason, many parents bathe their newborns in smaller areas like the sink and use plastic inserts to help keep the baby stationary while washing.

As your child gets older, the more likely locale for drowning risks are private pools, even small, plastic kiddie pools, hot tubs, etc. Even with this cautionary mentality, do not discount the danger of a bucket of water to a toddler when unsupervised.

Weak swimmers - It goes without saying that your baby cannot swim, to begin with. Even as they grow they will be weak in the water and can tire easily. On top of that, many adults report that they are not confident swimmers or very comfortable in the water, either.

If this is the case for you, don't worry, you can still have fun with your child in the water. Always make sure that you have the proper equipment such as flotation assistants for your child or life jackets when engaging in any deeper water for yourself and your child. Having another person present and on watch is also recommended.

Never leave your child unattended around any level of water that they could become submerged in, even just their head and face.

Non-Fatal Drownings - According to the CDC's (2022) statistics on drownings, one out of eight children die, the rest receiving emergency care. In these instances, drownings do not prove fatal, but can still have long-lasting effects on the victim.

Neurological disabilities are the primary injury noted in cases of non-fatal child drownings. It only takes a short time without oxygen to the brain to cause damage.

Substances and Medicine - Be very conscious of what medications you and your baby are taking when considering going for a swim. Any substance or medication that inhibits motor skills in any way, or affects balance, can be an added hazard. It should go without saying that the use of alcohol by parents when swimming with children can be a source of danger as well. Make sure there is someone who is designated to play lifeguard in any water-related fun.

HOUSEHOLD HAZARDS - ACCIDENTS AND EVERYDAY THREATS IN YOUR HOME

There are a lot of dangers that could befall your child, but this chapter is not meant to make you paranoid, or worry. We simply need to highlight the most common and often overlooked hazards for you to guard against and be able to set preventative measures for them.

Many dangers to your child might seem straightforward like electrical outlets and chemicals under the sink. You should, and probably already have installed baby-guarding locks and covers for those hazards. But there are quite a few that you may not be aware of.

Dishwashers - Similar to the washer and dryer, of course, you want to keep your little one from crawling into the machine. However, that is not the main source of worry where the dishwasher is concerned.

If you have a dishwasher in your home, you must be wary of:

Placing knives and forks down at their level. They may get a hold of a utensil and can cut or stab themselves. Not only that, but until they are washed, the dishes can be dirty and could make your child sick from licking them.

CHAPTER 6 | 121

Detergent is typically a bright, fun-looking color. This may seem attractive to your baby. Make sure you are careful to pour the liquid carefully.

Keep the door to the dishwasher closed and locked when not loading and unloading.

Latex Balloons - While this may appear to be an overly specific danger to mention, you will more than likely have balloons at your child's parties and events, or sometimes just get them for fun. There's a good reason for this: kids love balloons. They are bright and happy and a joy to play with.

Nonetheless, they are a choking hazard when they pop, or before they are inflated. Children may try to chew on the rubber, as well, which can lead to swallowing and choking. Your child will not have the proper lung capacity to blow up a balloon until they are around eight years old. This can lead to accidentally inhaling the rubber and suffocation (Parents Editors, 2009).

A full balloon may not present any significant worry to your child at any age, but if you are apprehensive, try buying mylar balloons instead. They are much bigger and less edible when they pop or deflate.

Oils and Shampoos - Like so many other products, take the time to identify yourself with what they contain. It doesn't take long to familiarize yourself with common ingredients. There are a few baby products that contain liquid hydrocarbons that can be harmful to your child if inhaled.

Doing your research will give you the peace of mind that the products you are purchasing and using on your baby are safe. It only takes a moment to read a label, and to store any moderately irritating or hazardous liquids properly and securely.

Pets - Dogs and Cats can injure young ones. Do not assume your pet will always be gentle with your baby. Even if they are, they can be pushed beyond the limits of their tolerance and patience. When they decide it's time to stop, it might mean they do it in the only way they know how to express their irritation.

Teeth and claws.

Teach your child about animal behavior. They should avoid a dog when it is eating and avoid teasing or cornering any animal.

Pet toys can also be choking hazards, and may potentially present a source of stress for your pet if your child takes them away whilst your pet is playing with the toys. Additionally, you may not want your kid chewing on the same toy that your dog just had in its mouth.

Power Windows in Cars - Motors are cool. Pushing buttons is entertaining and fascinating, especially when it has such a visual response, like power windows in cars. Make no mistake, those windows can cause a lot of damage to your child.

Your child could lose a finger or more if their extremities become trapped as the window closes. They might also get their head through the opening, becoming trapped around their neck. In the worst of these cases, they may suffer permanent injury to their windpipe and throat, or die from strangulation. Because of their size, a child can step on the button by mistake when moving to climb out the window.

Always apply the window lock on the driver-side panel until your children are old enough to responsibly control their own window and always remember to keep your child fastened securely in their car seat at all times when driving. This cannot be emphasized enough! Furthermore, never leave your child unattended in a vehicle for any reason. More on that in the next section.

The list goes on - We won't bog you down with the comprehensive list of every danger your child will encounter in life, but some other common hazards to highlight are:

- Leaving unattended purses or strangers' things out. When you have visitors, keep their items out of reach. Not everyone is cautious about what they carry in their bag. Your baby will explore.
- Be careful when acquiring used baby gear. Worn items may have sharp broken edges, frayed straps, and compromised structural integrity.
- Appliances tipping over. Little ones will climb. The oven is the most common pitfall. Keep the oven door locked and make sure the appliance's feet are adjusted for balance to avoid tipping and crushing. This will also prevent your child from becoming trapped inside the appliance.
- Climbing on shelves and drawers. The best way to keep them from doing this is to prevent them from accessing the kitchen. Baby gates are a must-have for controlling where your child can go.
- Power cords. Use cable management ties and systems to keep long cords from dangling. You don't want your child to become tangled in wires and choke.

HEATSTROKE - FORGETTING YOUR BABY IN THE CAR

You're exhausted. It's a hot day running to the store for something you forgot to pick up. You get out and head on in. Where is your baby?

It seems absurd to think you would forget something so important, but it happens too often. On average, 38 children die inside a hot car from heat stroke every year (Null, 2022).

Obviously, you cannot afford to let this happen.

While your baby is sleeping in their car seat in the back it's easy to get sidetracked and caught up in your thoughts of things you need to get done. Losing track of time and rushing is your number one enemy when it comes to unintentional negligence (A. Shaw, 2018).

Take a lesson on how serious the heat in a car can get. Many of us have watched the pet safety videos demonstrating someone testing this by waiting in a car on camera with the windows up. The message is clear. It's too hot for an adult to stand it for long. It's too hot for your pet, and it's absolutely too hot for your child.

To make absolutely sure you do not even take a chance of this happening, form habits that will keep you in check. Making a car exit routine is the first step to always remembering your child, there are several methods you can implement to practice safety:

- Set your phone in the back seat with them. You will hunt for your phone before you get out.
- Practice checking the back seat every time you get out of the car. Walk a circle around your car every time you get out for good measure.
- Talk to your baby on your drive time. This will keep them at the forefront of your thoughts.
- If you are dropping your child off, have the sitter or daycare call you to remind you on your way or at a certain time if the child has not arrived. Parents often forget and autopilot to work with the child still in the back.
- Place one of their toys in the passenger seat as a reminder.
- There are apps and tech to remind you when you go to get out of your car to not forget the baby. Try downloading one from your preferred app store.

Statistics from the United States over the past twenty years document the prominent causes of heatstroke. Sadly, more than 50% of these deaths were caused by simple forgetfulness (Null, 2022).

In 25% of cases, the child gained access to the vehicle by themselves. Let this be a reminder to always know where your child is, and where your keys are. Keep the car locked even at home in the garage.

Unfortunately, 20% are due to neglect or committed knowingly by a caregiver. There is never an excuse for these preventable deaths and those parents have to suffer the permanent loss of their baby and in many cases legal charges and jail time (Null, 2022).

It's your job and duty to prevent harm from coming to your child.

RUNAWAY STROLLERS - NOT USING THE BRAKES

Another common danger facing parents and children is also car-related, in a way. Strollers can get away from you on a hill, or in a windy or sloping parking lot. More often than not, if the stroller starts rolling you will see it, jump for it, and catch it. But every once in a while parents miss it. Even when it doesn't result in harm to the child, you cannot let this happen.

It's far too easy to forget to use the brake every time you stop to chat, check your phone, or tie your shoelace...

A driver might not see the stroller until it is too late (Shadwell, 2020). There are few statistics around car collision/stroller-related fatalities in babies, but any number is too high. Make this another safety habit in your daily routine with your baby. Stay alert at all times when in higher-risk situations and normal everyday scenarios.

- Make the habit of using the brake EVERY TIME YOU STOP, for any reason. Hill or no hill.
- Stay present and don't let distractions take your mind off of your child and keep track of them.
- Many strollers come with a wrist strap. Use it, or get one to use. It cannot get away from you if it is attached to you.

If you do have a scare, don't worry. You are not the first or the last parent to have this happen. Talk to other parents about it and get support and encouragement to do better and insight on how to manage your stroller better.

SLEEPING WITH YOUR BABY

DO NOT fall asleep holding your baby. Under no circumstances is it a good idea to lay them with you in your bed, or on the couch when you might fall asleep. It can result in suffocation and smothering your child.

Although strides have been made to raise awareness of SIDS (Sudden Infant Death Syndrome) and to educate and identify the causes of it in recent years, 3500 babies and infants still die each year from related causes. Suffocations and strangulations, however, have increased. Around 28% of the infant deaths reported each year are due to this cause. That's 960 children in the US alone (US Department of Health, 2021).

Remember that your baby has no way to move themselves or alert you if they wind up in a compromised position. They may cry out, but you should not rely on this.

We'll circle back to staying mindful and alert repeatedly when it comes to child safety. You are the front line of danger prevention when it comes to your baby.

Make it a point any time you feel like you might nod off to go put them in their crib or bed and find a place to take a nap, even if it's in the nursery with them. If you are worried about slipping off to sleep, try only holding your baby standing up as long as you are too tired, or sitting in a chair you are not likely to get comfortable in.

- You will be tired a lot. Don't let that lower your guard.
- On the couch, they could slip down between the cushions or get pinned between you and the backrest.
- In bed, your infant might roll onto their face in your comforter or covers and suffocate.
- Too many parents swear that they don't move around when they sleep, but this is too big of a risk to take while you are unconscious.
- Even just occasionally taking a nap with your baby is still a big risk. The only time it is safe to nap with your child is when another adult, parent, or friend is in the room watching you. And not just checking in periodically. Have a spotter at all times.
- If you decide to try co-sleeping, having your baby in your room, always use an attachment to your bed or a bedside crib, but never let your baby sleep in the bed with you.

Takeaway Tips:

- Stay alert for signs of neglect so you can be proactive in defusing harmful situations your family might fall into.
- Some situations can have severe and sometimes fatal consequences for you and your child.
- Make a habit of checking your car, even when the kids aren't in it with you.
- Use reminder techniques every time you ride with your little one in the car.
- Employ a wrist strap and use the pram brake on your stroller every time you stop.
- Never let go of the stroller in high-risk environments like parking lots and hills.
- Never take a nap alone holding your baby. Never.

7

TEAMWORK MAKES THE DREAM WORK

All first-time dads feel a unique burden of responsibility for providing care for their children. Without meaning to, you may find yourself trying to take on too much, and not consulting or working in concert with your child's mother.

This mistake can be costly for both parents in a variety of ways, from feeling isolated and overworked to feeling left out or neglected. You have already seen some of the consequences of this kind of behavior in relation to other aspects of parenting and your relationship with your partner.

You will each need to find and develop your roles and your strengths in parenting for your baby. This means using open and thorough communication and teamwork.

Ultimately your child will thrive when the two of you can work well as a parental unit, and both parents will find individual benefits, as well.

"SHARING IS CARING"- NOT DEVELOPING A SHARED MENTALITY WITH MOM

No two people can see eye to eye on every subject all the time. That does not mean that you can't find compromises and make decisions that everyone can be content with. You must meet somewhere in the middle to successfully parent your child.

To reach that point, you will have to work on establishing a shared mentality. It's more than just an agreement, but a system of long-term decisions, rules, and ongoing discussions about how you want to raise your child. Division of labor and a team-oriented game plan is key to finding balance.

Teamwork only develops with practice. You or your partner might make the better coach, but ideally, the two of you will both bring different aspects of leadership to the relationship needed to benefit your child. Developing the skills of checking with one another, staying mindful of the things that need to get done, and not just your own, can prevent small problems like missed appointments, to huge problems that may endanger your relationship with your child or the mother.

First, it's important to look at the foundation of what you need to succeed, and common hurdles that parents run into that you may not think of until you encounter them.

Mental Models - In industry, mental models refer to perceptions of what a project should look like, what level of quality and features it should have, and an overall purpose for the product in question. Fallouts in mental model perspectives across a team result in costly redesigns and mis-marketing, just to name a few of the problems (Goff-Dupont, 2021). Now apply the same principle to parenting. Think of how it affects your relationship with your partner. Miscommunication, unnecessary conflicts, and frustration arise from a failed team mentality in parenting.

Successful mental models for teams are built from the ground up with everyone in mind. This is exactly what we have been talking about. Several factors play into a prosperous mental model that can benefit the way you think of your parenting team:

- Team health. Not just physically, but the way the team works. What does your ideal teamwork look like? How can you make it work better?
- Clearly defined duties. Who does what? When? How?
- Establish quality control. What you consider "good" might not meet your partner's standards. Find a middle ground. Set the bar for expectations.

These team-building tactics can provide you with some very useful tools to get along with your partner and tackle the tasks you have to accomplish. Apply just some of these constructive approaches to your partnership and see how much better you work together.

Going it Alone - Previously we mentioned not letting the mother take on every task alone. This does not mean that you have to do everything as the father, either. Parenting is a balance.

Trying to juggle everything is simply too much for one person to handle without some serious energy and organization. We have stressed how important seeking out help is to make it through the first few months, and the rest of your child's upbringing.

Outside help aside, one of the biggest mistakes along these lines is not dividing the work between each other as parents. Understandably, this may not be possible for all situations if one partner is no longer in the picture, but this should never become an issue when both parents are present and available.

Whether it's due to neglect or apathy on the part of one parent, or one person's inability to relinquish control, the weight can drag any single person down eventually. The results can be resentment, exhaustion, and most importantly, failures to meet the needs of your children.

Take the time to sit down and have planning and assignment discussions. It may seem formal and a bit silly to have business meetings with your partner, but setting up the structure and division of labor will prevent single-mindedness and dropping the ball.

Staff Meeting - Set a time each week to touch base with each other. The discussion does not have to be long, but having dedicated time for problem-solving and reaching agreements about matters from the trivial to the most serious issues is a must for stability and crisis aversion. This communication can and should extend to your children as they get older. Make them a part of the process for small things at first and bigger ones as they grow. They don't need to be present for heavy matters of parenting but showing them the way you make plans as a team will help them develop important life skills such as teamwork, problem-solving, and planning ahead.

Flexibility - The mistake here really has more to do with the opposite. Being inflexible comes back to give and take, and compromise. Be willing to listen. Give constructive criticism and be open to receiving it. No one wants to work with someone who won't budge on any issue.

On the other side of the coin, be flexible about your flexibility. Being the partner willing to jump on whatever needs doing and picking up any slack is immensely helpful, especially if mom is overwhelmed. Also, be ready to take cues from your child's mother if she has specific ways she wants to go about things. You can take charge when the need arises, but sometimes it's best to go with the flow.

Use all of the tools you've learned so far to stay calm and bring a level and solid support to every parenting situation, whether you take the lead, or your partner does.

Playing to Strengths - Duties, and responsibilities will not always be a 50/50 split in the real world. The most important factor is to decide together who will be best suited to handle a task rather than trying to equally divide everything. Understanding strengths and weaknesses will have the right person making dinner and the right person helping with the homework.

Everyone has areas they excel in and others where they could improve. There are also some areas we all know that we generally steer clear of because we just aren't good at them. But that can be one of the best parts about there being two parents in a child's life. Trade off!

This doesn't need to be overly specific either. You do not have to make an encyclopedia of tasks and who is better at each. However, if your partner is a more talented public speaker than you are, let them take the lead at a school event and offer your support in other ways.

Of course, if both of you struggle with an ability or activity, one of you may have to suck it up and do some learning or training to fill that void of need. Your child will inevitably bring some math homework to you or ask you to show them a sports maneuver that neither of you has a clue about, but figuring it out together can be a fun part of being a parent, too!

To Each, Their Own - Individual parents all have their own styles and methods of handling discipline, rewards, and many other day-to-day interactions with their children. On a few of these fronts, you must be united for consistency and to present a solid shelter of unity for your children to thrive under.

Nevertheless, you are each your own person. Where your child's mother may be an expert advice-giver in certain situations, you may be the parent who excels at listening and offering a shoulder to cry on. Even more subtly, each of you will have quirks in the way you do things, and neither of them is wrong or right.

Your children will cherish the way you made their breakfast just as much as they appreciate the way their mother did it in her own way. Once you have set the stage for the major themes with your partner, you can let your creativity and individuality shine within those boundaries as a parent.

Mental Strain - There are innumerable tasks that fall outside the normal and everyday upkeep of the home and family needs. Making doctor's appointments, communicating with other parents about sleepovers, looking over grades and homework, and planning and researching activities such as summer trips are hard to quantify, but they take a toll in terms of workload, time, and mental energy.

We've all spent far too long on hold with customer service and understand the toll it takes on our patience and mental fortitude.

This type of logistical and complex labor is harder to divide up. Often, the majority of it falls to the stay-at-home parent, if there is one. Unfortunately, it can end up wearing down the parent who has to handle most of it. These more ambiguous tasks need to be equally assigned to avoid burnout.

To better understand the issue, think of how your parents had a certain way they wanted some things done. Maybe your mom always wanted the dishes put away just so, or your dad insisted on cleaning things in a particular order. While a lot of it is simply preference, it still taxes your available energies if you are the one making all of those calls on how things get done.

In addition to the thought put into details and execution, a lot of learning goes into getting things done. Someone has to take the time to watch the tutorial video or read your child's textbook to remember how to help them with the class material. Those are just a couple of examples of yet more drains on your cognitive resources.

Remember, you have been studying how to be a better learner and teacher. Offer to be the one who does the research or finds the repairman's number if your partner is the one who seems to deal with these things most often.

Be careful not to be overly controlling or uncompromising, or you can more easily find yourself doing it all. Your partner won't want to assist if you are too demanding.

Priorities - We've come full circle back to one of the topics addressed in the earlier chapters. Now you should be able to see it in a new light with everything else you have learned. Prioritizing isn't just a list of goals and desires for major life choices and decisions. When you have limited time and resources it must also encompass mundane necessities and chores.

Especially at the start when your child is a baby, you will need every available moment for sleep and seeing to their needs. As they begin to become somewhat independent of your constant attention, you can begin to add priorities back to your repertoire. The one benefit of trimming the fat is that when you do start to get back to things, you will realize what is necessary and what is not.

Each parent may have a different view of what is a must and what isn't. That is where communication and compromise come in once more to settle the score. It does not take much effort or much time to simply ask what your partner would prefer and offer your own suggestions.

Treating your to-dos with the importance they deserve helps them hold gravity and meaning, and ultimately, will ensure that you do them. Along with shared communication mediums for contact, download a task app or list creation app. Something even as simple as Google Calendars that allows the two of you to leave notes on tasks and see exactly what you have going on any given day and week. A shared calendar or list is much more permanent than a call or text and can always be referenced (Jacobs, 2020).

Appreciation and Gratitude - Just like you need to speak up when things aren't right, or when you need to decide who is going to vacuum or take out the trash, you should also get into the habit of saying thank you. A little gratitude goes a long way. And it promotes positivity all around. Failure to show appreciation can cause undue strain on your relationship.

ASSUMPTIONS - COMFORTING AND TOUGH

Mom Mojo - There is a thin line between playing to your strengths and assuming what each one of you should be doing in your roles as parents. A lot of it comes from tropes in media, stereotypes, and outdated role culture.

Moms typically have a reputation for being the compassionate ones, the comforters, and the primary caregivers. It is also assumed that Dads do not usually have those qualities. We know this is silly, to attribute those traits only to mothers when fathers can also have those qualities.

What follows from those same assumptions, are the archetypes forced on dads. Similar to assumptions that a woman should know how to sew, there's the idea that every dad knows how to fix plumbing or a car. We know these things are not true and can be harmful to expectations.

Just like how you know by now that you are just as loving and capable of providing your child with comfort and care, as well as their fundamental needs, you may still encounter those who think dads aren't cut out for it. We may have exposed some of the myths and stereotypes for what they are, but there are still a lot of opinions out there that endorse that line of thinking.

Fortunately, that won't phase you or stop you from doing what you need to do for your family. We would not give you all of these warnings and stumbling blocks without the information you need to overcome them.

Solid Defense - When uncomfortable, foolish, or biased comments happen, you need a good response. Establishing new norms in parenting will require facing some of the stereotypes and misconceptions we mentioned previously.

- Dad is not babysitting the kids. He's parenting.
- Mom is not filling in by taking them camping.
- Dad is not *helping out*. He is doing his share of the work.
- Mom isn't abandoning the kids when she leaves them with him.

Within your circles, you must set the stage for what people expect and how you expect them to respect your methods of parenting.

Outside the family, maintaining a cohesive outlook also lets others know how to approach you and your children. When it comes to doctors, family members, and friends, if you are firm on your parameters, you are less likely to encounter uncomfortable situations and disagreements. Teachers working with parents find that children tend to perform better when there is a shared mentality on the home front, even in cases of upheavals such as divorce (Our Family Wizard, 2021).

BEING PROACTIVE - GETTING AHEAD OF THE CURVE AND STAYING PREPARED

Without Being Told - One of the biggest mistakes that add considerable frustration to the mental load of parenting is having to also constantly remind everyone of their chores. We have all been guilty of it at one point or another with family, friends, or work.

"Tell me what needs to be done and I'll do it."

There is still a responsibility and task involved in having to remind someone of what they already agreed to do in sharing the to-do list. Doing the task also involves any learning involved with and the initiative to get it done so that it is completely your duty and yours alone.

Presence - More involvement begets more involvement. Making time to appear at events and appointments will encourage you and your partner to continue to do so. It may mean taking turns or requiring some scheduling to make it work, but the more you stay in the loop on all matters of your child's life, the more you will keep it up and want to.

Neglect can take root when you fall behind and feel left out of some aspects of childhood development. Remember, you don't want to get sidelined or let yourself fade into the background of your children's lives. Stay active, interested, and informed.

In-contact - Each parent should be as reachable as the other, and both need to have interaction with your child's everyday encounters: friends and their parents or administrative figures like teachers and doctors.

Dealing directly with lines of communication, think about setting up an email that both parents have access to for child-related contacts. This is just one of many ideas that help to dispel the scenario of one parent receiving all of the calls, all of the correspondence from school, and approving medical appointments and follow-ups.

THE SHARED MINDSET - TEAMWORK AND COMMUNICATION

All of this finally brings us to the culmination of the subject which is the shared mindset you want to reside in with your partner. It will take time and effort to build your routine into habits and hopefully, a new lifestyle of constant communication and productivity.

Once you understand what it's like to work in this positive and informative environment, you won't want it to ever go back to the way it was, and it can be beneficial to the rest of your life in how it influences you to stay organized.

Keep referring back to this list to make sure you are staying on track:

- Ask about your partner's mental workload. Share yours with them.
- Have scheduled team meetings. Planned communication puts added importance on it.
- Set goals and always be updating whose responsibilities belong to whom.
- Keep a calendar or listing app that you can both check into and comment on.
- Stay proactive and always be updating and learning.

Before long, you will start to really feel like an efficient team. And speaking of teamwork, once you reach that level, there are some finer points to grow on to reinforce your new routine.

UPKEEP - HEALTHY PARENTAL RELATIONSHIPS

Leading up to the delivery and the few months after will fly by in a blur, and it's easy to lose track of time and of paying attention to anything but your infant.

During this time and the busy years to come, you have to find ways to keep your relationships afloat and preferably thriving alongside your new life. It may seem daunting, but it is well worth the effort.

Don't let one of the most important people in your life slip down the priority list. Regardless of the nature of your relationship with your child's mother, now more than ever, you will need each other's support.

We have alluded to this topic previously, but now it's time to delve into it in-depth and provide some guidance on ways to maintain a relationship with your partner or co-parent.

All of the aforementioned suggestions still apply: follow the Takeaway Tips and reread them from time to time for good pointers. Many of them will translate to this section as well.

Openness - This is just another reminder to communicate. This includes but is not limited to your roles and responsibilities as parents. You also have a real relationship to maintain with your partner. Replacing your identity as a couple with only the identity of parents can cause irreparable damage to your relationship. You must integrate the two aspects of your partnership.

We cannot stress enough how frank and candid conversation can have such an impact on the outcome of a relationship. Share your feelings. Establish and provide a safe and accepting environment in which to exchange concerns, commentary, and insecurity.

When the time comes for negotiating or compromising, you don't want there to be distance or a divide between you. Always forgive easily, thank freely, and be kind with what you say.

Planning - All of your organization and careful planning should win you more rewards than just a smooth daily routine. Setting aside time for a date night, or just time alone together is important. You don't have to do anything fancy. The idea is to just continue the relationship that you had before your baby came along and keep it alive in its own right, not simply as a coordinated structure for your child's benefit.

Have fun. Do activities together. Talk. And don't let some sort of intimate behavior fall to the wayside, either.

Intimacy - Although sex is important in a relationship and plays a key role in intimacy, it isn't the only form. Intimacy can also include other physical forms such as cuddling on the couch, showing affection with hugs and kisses, or even just holding hands. Past the obvious forms that we acknowledge, intimacy can also be experiences shared, emotional moments, and intellectual sharing of knowledge and conversation.

It's important to consider what your partner responds to best, whether it's physical affection, gifts, verbal affirmation, considerate gestures, or just time spent with them. This will help you cater to their needs, and they can better understand yours in the same way.

Part of the issue with a lack of intimacy following the birth of a child is energy. When all you want to do is lay down and go to sleep, you hardly feel like getting intimate with your partner. Aside from sexual intimacy, this extends to gestures of appreciation and time spent together romantically and for fun. When you are depleted, you don't think of picking up a gift or doing something kind for your partner. Eventually, this can lead to feeling distant from your significant other.

Growing distant from your partner is a slow and sometimes subtle process. It's up to you to make an effort to keep it going.

CO-PARENTING

If your child's mother is not your partner, for whatever reason, the situation can have a slew of obstacles and uncomfortable challenges. Fortunately, using many of the same teamwork techniques mentioned before can alleviate a lot of the discomfort. Children in these situations tend to be negatively affected by unpleasant interactions on the part of the parents, but it doesn't have to be that way.

Whether from divorce or if you were never together in a relationship with your child's mother to begin with, you will have to work with them if you want to be in your child's life.

Modifying the methods used to maintain your relationship with your partner can have just as much of an effect:

- Communicate directly with the mother. Not through the kids. You will need to be very clear and consistent when communicating with your child's mother.
- Disagree privately. Just like communicating directly with the mom, always address concerns immediately, and not in front of the kids.
- Keep exchanges amicable and concise.
- Documentation. Keep a record of interactions and agreements with the mother for accountability and transparency.
- Stick to the script. Make the same decisions you would as a couple parenting about your child's life and don't deviate.

- Make a schedule and stick to it. If your weekends are spent with your kids, don't switch things up too much, and always give ample warning when you have to make changes. Furthermore, always put your children's schedules first. Every child needs and has the right to consistency and stability in their lives.
- You can still employ a mutual calendar to share your schedules and stay on the same page.

At the end of the day, there will be mistakes you cannot avoid when dealing with your partner or the mother of your child, but you now have the tools necessary to mitigate the majority of them with a little forethought and discipline.

Takeaway Tips:

- Examine all of the tasks that you and your partner need to do and fairly assign them.
- Be willing to make compromises and wholeheartedly get behind those decisions once they are made.
- Communicate openly and regularly with your partner or your child's mother.
- Play off and take advantage of each other's strengths.

- Practice efficient teamwork. Support each other.
- Remember to show gratitude and appreciation.
- Show off your shared mentality! Defy expectations.
- Make time for you and your partner. Every relationship needs attention or it can fall apart.
- Co-parenting can work. Set aside your differences and work with the mother for the sake of the life you created together.

8

WE'RE ONLY HUMAN

All of the chapters so far have built upon each other to warn you about the mistakes you will potentially make in your newfound fatherhood. They have also been cumulatively giving you tools to solve all of those problems and prevent most of them. Many of your mistakes and their solutions overlap. Sometimes they may pile up and feel like they will overwhelm you, other times you may find solving multiple issues only requires one blanket fix.

Regardless of the severity or quality of the hurdle, you are perfectly capable of handling all of it. But possibly the most important lesson to learn at the end of all of it is that you are human. We all are. Sure, you can say it a thousand times, but you need to truly accept and believe it to become a great father.

Otherwise, you will not be able to accept your flaws and your misconceptions or eliminate them. This final chapter deals with personal mistakes we make as parents. We can't always get it right, but accepting that is just as important as fixing the problems and moving on. None of us are perfect, but if we learn from our mistakes then we can all be amazing parents!

PARENTAL BOO-BOOS

Beating yourself up about every little thing will do you no good. Taking your slips and falls into consideration and learning from them will. Remember to extend the kindness you give to others, to your kids and your partner, to yourself.

Workaholic - This is not a new struggle. Dads have a reputation for working too much, and not being home enough, missing events, not spending quite enough time with their children. Movies and television have added to this stigma.

However, you aren't a villain or a failure for working too much, even if it makes you feel like one. Dad-guilt and mom-guilt are real things. Either parent can feel like they are not around enough, torn between their job and spending time with their kids. Really looking at your priorities can be the catalyst for you to make a call to rearrange your schedule.

Don't let this overwhelm you. There will be times when you have to work more than you would like. The important thing is to not be too hard on yourself or let guilt overcome you. It's safe to say most parents want more time with their kids, and in reality, only you will know your circumstances and what is ultimately necessary to see to the needs of your family and your goals. The best thing to do is to carefully weigh whether you should work those extra hours, or set that time aside for your family. Have regular reviews and assess your circumstances.

Breaking Promises - We all have throughout our lives, and you will again with your child. With realistic expectations and focused analysis of your schedule and your capacity, make every effort to only commit to what you know you can do.

Try not to set the bar too high by making big statements of certainty. Be honest. Make every effort to show up, to follow through. And when you do fail and break a promise, do everything in your power not to let it happen again and to make up for it.

Taking A Break - Or to put it more accurately, NOT taking enough breaks. When you are stressed and overwrought with tasks and meeting the needs of your family, you need to take time aside. Do not feel guilty for refilling your reservoirs with time alone. If you don't it can lead to emotional exhaustion and harmful behaviors like neglect and a lack of self-care.

Many of the signs that you need a break are very similar to mistakes we have covered previously, but these behaviors can be a result of burnout, as well. If you notice that you are struggling to sleep, have trouble controlling your emotions and outbursts, are judging yourself too harshly, or are starting to neglect your parental duties and everyday tasks, it means you need time to recuperate.

Being Bigger - When you mess up, there is only one thing to do. Apologize. To your partner *and* to your kids.

Your children are people and they have feelings. Showing humility and the ability to accept your mistakes and learn from them is one of the most important lessons you can teach them. Admitting your flaws openly whilst also addressing and working on them will earn you a lot of respect from your family. And it will show them that, they too, can make mistakes, and that it's all about learning from them. Every mistake is a learning opportunity and a chance to teach your kids a lesson through your actions. This is what role-modeling is: developing and evolving.

Forgiving Yourself - Possibly the most imperative rule for surviving as a father, and as a human being, is to learn how to forgive yourself.

You cannot truly treat others with compassion and mercy, or teach those qualities to your children if you're not applying them in your own life. And as we all know, if you do not forgive yourself and make the necessary changes to the behavior, you will most likely repeat it.

Your kids have half of who you are in them. They will be prone to many of the same traits that you have and tend to handle them the same way, more so from watching how you react in similar situations.

Forgiving yourself is especially important when it comes to things that are out of your control. In life, there are so many things that are not in your control, no matter how much you might prepare for them. You must learn how to accept those things and cope with them when they are out of your hands. When you encounter these types of situations, focus on the things you can control, set new goals, and reassess what you should expect, to get a better perspective.

That all but covers just about every common mistake that you will encounter as a new dad. The next time you find yourself up against a stumbling block, take a minute to look at this list to help you navigate:

- Identify and recognize the error.
- Try to understand and explain how and why it happened.
- Say you're sorry. That means acknowledging, verbalizing, and *showing* you are sorry.
  Changing your behavior is the truest form of apology.
- Talk about what happened.
- Take notes and learn from your mistakes.
- Turn the lesson into action. Change it.
- Don't dwell on it. Move forward and don't repeat it

(All Pro Dad, 2014).

The last thing that needs to be covered is the most personal. Addressing your mental and emotional state is something you need to do regularly and should be faced head-on.

MIND AND BODY - RESTING AND MENTAL HEALTH

Hand in hand with forgiving comes being kind to yourself. That involves taking care of your body and mind. If you've learned one thing through reading this book is that you need sleep and well-being to meet the needs of your new baby.

Depression - One in ten dads suffers from depression (Cadbury, 2021). There are so many things that can cause it from sleep deprivation, to work stress, or feeling excluded from maternity and infancy concerns.

First, it's critical to understand that it is not your fault if you start to feel this way. Chemical imbalances are very real, and not discussed enough. It is a fairly complex topic and you should be aware of how they can contribute to depression (Harvard Health, 2022). Chemical imbalances in your brain chemistry can lead to a variety of issues from long-term anxiety to depression and other mental and emotional conditions. More often than not they are a result of multiple factors like stress, sleep deprivation, grief, or life-altering circumstances.

Depression is more common than most people think, and though you may start to feel isolated in sadness or dark thoughts, remember that you are not alone.

Second, what you do with these feelings will mean everything. You are capable of getting the help you need. Do not let pride or apathy win out over seeking assistance.

Separation Anxiety - Closely related to inner turmoil, and often a contributing factor to dads' depression is a sense that he is not getting the chance to bond with his new baby (Ceder, 2021). This extends to the relationship with their partner and feeling a decline in closeness.

To add to the strain, time constraints and scheduling can also make it very difficult to spend time with friends and other family members. Isolation and overextending are very real dangers in parenting.

These feelings are sometimes just part of the journey and will pass once things settle into a routine where you can get back in touch with those around you. However, trying to stay in contact and making time for the people in your life is the only way to keep from being cut off or overwhelmed. You need support. Babysitters to give you a break, friends, and mentors to talk to.

Prevention - Doing everything you can to prevent emotional and mental decline during and after pregnancy is your first line of defense. Do all of the things you know are good for your brain and body to stay as healthy as you can leading up to the big day.

- Get enough sleep. We may have mentioned this a couple of thousand times throughout this book. Sleep is the best healer, the best energy giver, and one of the most important contributors to your mental health.
- Eat right. Make healthy and nutritious meals to fuel your body. You will need plenty of energy to sustain you through the difficult days ahead. The mealtime routine should be kept to as much as possible to ensure that you don't miss meals and crash when you need to be alert.
- Exercise. Your body performs better when you use it properly. Exercise relieves stress, promotes good hormone production, increases energy, and prevents disease.
- Indulge in pastimes and pleasures. It is vital to stay in tune with your hobbies and other interests that you enjoy beyond your identity as a father. Keep those sources of inspiration, they are fuel for personal joy.

Getting the right help - The first step in getting any help is simply acknowledging that you need it. Next is deciding what kind of help you need and how to go about getting it.

Along with your planning and organization, look into options and support systems in the case that you end up in a less than optimal state of mind. Talking to your doctor about the possibilities can be very informative, and it also keeps them informed of your current state. It allows them to be on the lookout for possible signs of mental struggles.

Awareness is the best ally when it comes to any mental health concerns. That leads to the next warning alert which involves communicating your worries to your partner and to your friends. Have them keep a close eye on your behavior and your mood during times of high stress.

There are also various tools at your disposal such as online blogs and communities of other dads to talk to. Sometimes being able to unload your concerns anonymously can help to purge a lot of worry.

Similarly, but more professionally, there are apps like the Baby Buddy app and help crisis lines that you can call to speak with someone about your problems. Any way you go about it, the main thing is to find a healthy outlet and get support. You can't remain in the darkness. You have a family that needs you.

HOW TO BE BETTER - REFLECTING ON EVERYTHING YOU'VE LEARNED

From the first moment you heard that you were going to be a dad, you have started learning. Likely even before that, you had thoughts of the kind of dad you would want to be one day, of how your choices would affect your children, and of how your own history with your father would influence how you would or wouldn't do things. You are not your father. That doesn't mean you should not try to emulate those good qualities you learned from him, or that you won't sometimes falter and mimic the faults that he passed on to you. Ultimately, you are your own man and you are not bound to repeat any mistake your parents made.

You might reflect on each and every decision you make as your baby starts their life. The choices you make will define them in many ways. Stay alert and process useful information to be ever learning and ever growing into a better parent.

The key is to assess your own burdens and issues and do everything you can to heal and not pass those hurts on to your children. Make adjustments to your behavior and your methods of parenting.

While you reflect on how you are growing, it pays to remind yourself that throughout the pregnancy, the birth, infancy, toddler years, and beyond, the good will outweigh the bad. Instead of more warnings, here are a few helpful reminders to help you be all the dad you can be:

- Just do your best, it's all about effort.
- Love. Love. Love your kid.
- Talk to them. Share.
- Try to let humor lighten the mood. Laugh.
- Celebrate. Even when there's no reason to. Especially then!
- Use positive reinforcement with yourself and others!
- Spend as much time with your child as you possibly can.

Do your research, take precautions, make preparations and learn from your mistakes.

The only Takeaway Tip here is don't worry too much! Trust your abilities and the love of your child. You're going to be an amazing dad.

FINAL WORDS

There is no ready-made, microwave solution to turn you into the perfect father. Becoming the ideal parent for your child is a journey. It's exciting, captivating, and a worthwhile challenge. Now, however, you have all of the know-how to avoid falling victim to those typical mistakes, big or small.

Each time you sidestep one of the boo-boos mentioned in this book, you are one step closer to being a better dad. Make the necessary and instrumental changes in your life. Knowledge is power and you have all of the tools and insights you need to gain confidence and build on what you know.

Managing your routine and your time both at work and at home starts with organization. You will get frustrated and impatient in your role as a dad, but you now have the tools to mitigate those feelings and healthily process them without taking them out on your child or partner. All of the misconceptions out there, and the assumptions you may have had have been put to rest, and you have seen enough to be able to pick out any we didn't cover and handle them accordingly. Knowing exactly what your role is, both the chosen duties and the expected responsibilities gives you a clear and defined purpose.

When trials arise around you, or within you, you will be alert to the dangers of emotional and psychological distress as well as being prepared to address any threats to your child. Being aware and knowledgeable is your best defense against harm coming to you or your baby.

You have come a long way in a short period of time, but the changes are just getting started. Now that you have all of the tools, you have everything you need to get the job done and how to assist the baby's mother. Do not worry about everything that could go wrong, you can't really anticipate everything that will happen with your partner and child. The best thing you can do is prepare and try your best.

You are going to be a great dad.

There are many resources out there. Use them to keep growing. Take the lessons in this book with you and share it with other up-and-coming dads. Put their minds at ease.

If you found this book useful, please leave a review on Amazon to help other first-time fathers benefit too.

All that's left after that is to go spend some time with your kids. Read to them, laugh with them, and play with them while they are still little. Time flies, but you will always have the memories spent with your children.

And they will have a lifetime of joy spent with the best dad they ever could have asked for.

REFERENCES

10 Absolutely Crucial Time Management Tips for Dads." 2017. Fatherly. October 26, 2017. https://www.fatherly.com/love-money/time-management-tips-dads/

All Pro Dad. (2014, July 19). *7 Ways to Recover from Your Parenting Mistakes*. Retrieved May 17, 2022, from https://www.allprodad.com/7-ways-to-recover-from-your-parenting-mistakes/

American SPCC. (2022, February 24). *Child Maltreatment & Neglect Statistics | American SPCC - Effects of Parental Alcohol Abuse*. Retrieved May 30, 2022, from https://americanspcc.org/child-maltreatment-statistics/

BHE Team. (2021, June 15). *How to Be a Good Father: Tips & Advice for Dads*. Bright Horizons. Retrieved April 18, 2022, from https://www.brighthorizons.com/family-resources/the-art-of-being-a-father

Brown, J. (2021, July 19). *How to Truly Share the Mental Load in a Marriage, According to Five Therapists*. Fatherly. Retrieved May 16, 2022, from https://www.fatherly.com/love-money/how-to-share-mental-load-marriage/

Child Welfare Information Gateway. (2019). Long-term consequences of child abuse and neglect. Washington, DC: U.S. Department of Health and Human Services, Administration for Children and Families, Children's Bureau.

C.S. Mott Children's Hospital. (2019, June 12). *Parenting put-downs: How criticism impacts fathers.* National Poll on Children's Health. Retrieved April 13, 2022, from https://mottpoll.org/reports/parenting-put-downs-how-criticism-impacts-fathers

Cadbury, N. (2021, December 29). *Looking after fathers' mental health.* Best Beginnings. Retrieved May 17, 2022, from https://www.bestbeginnings.org.uk/blog/looking-after-fathers-mental-health

Ceder, J. (2021, March 25). *Dads Struggle With Postpartum Depression Too.* Verywell Family. Retrieved May 26, 2022, from https://www.verywellfamily.com/dads-struggle-with-postpartum-depression-4023009

Centers for Disease Control. (2022, March 10). *Drowning Facts | Drowning Prevention | CDC.* CDC. Retrieved June 6, 2022, from https://www.cdc.gov/drowning/facts/index.html

Centers for Disease Control. (2022a, April 6). *Fast Facts: Preventing Child Abuse & Neglect |Violence Prevention|Injury Center|CDC.* CDC.-Gov. Retrieved May 30, 2022, from https://www.cdc.gov/violenceprevention/childabuseandneglect/fastfact.html

ChoosingTherapy.com. (2022, April 4). *Overprotective Parents: Signs, Examples, & Impact on Mental Health.* Choosing Therapy. Retrieved April 18, 2022, from https://www.choosingtherapy.com/overprotective-parents/

Costa, Gina. 2005. "15 Time-Management Tips." Parents. Parents. October 3, 2005. https://www.parents.com/parenting/moms/healthy-mom/time-management-tips/

Dad Gold. (2021, June 29). *7 Tips You Can Use To Develop New Dad Patience*. Retrieved April 13, 2022, from https://dadgold.com/new-dad-patience/

Domestikated Life. (2017, March 29). *Tips for Researching Baby Gear*. Retrieved April 18, 2022, from https://domestikatedlife.-com/2017/03/29/tips-for-researching-baby-gear/

Early Learning. (2018, July 5). *Why reading with Dad matters | First Five Years*. First Five Years. Retrieved April 18, 2022, from https://www.firstfiveyears.org.au/early-learning/why-reading-with-dad-matters

Fuller, J. (2022, April 4). *First-Time Dads: Learning From Your Father's Mistakes*. Focus on the Family. Retrieved May 17, 2022, from https://www.focusonthefamily.com/parenting/first-time-dads-learning-from-your-fathers-mistakes/

Gallie, M. (2014, January 28). *11 strategies to stop a toddler from running away in public*. BabyCenter LLC. Retrieved April 16, 2022, from https://www.babycenter.ca/a1040641/11-strategies-to-stop-a-toddler-from-running-away-in-public

Garcia, N. (2021, December 26). *Why You Shouldn't Tell Your Child to Stop Crying*. Sleeping Should Be Easy. Retrieved April 18, 2022, from https://sleepingshouldbeeasy.com/stop-crying/

Gidick, K. (2021, January 6). *6 Signs You Need A Healthy Break From Your Kids, According To Experts*. Romper. Retrieved May 31, 2022, from https://www.romper.com/parenting/signs-you-need-a-healthy-break-from-your-kids-according-to-experts

Goff-Dupont, S. (2021, January 21). *How to boost your team's success with shared mental models*. Work Life by Atlassian. Retrieved May 16,

2022, from https://www.atlassian.com/blog/teamwork/shared-mental-models-improve-team-performance

Haas, M., & Mortensen, M. (2022, March 30). *The Secrets of Great Teamwork*. Harvard Business Review. Retrieved May 16, 2022, from https://hbr.org/2016/06/the-secrets-of-great-teamwork

Happy. (2019, June 25). *The Importance of Seeking Help*. HIF. Retrieved April 18, 2022, from https://blog.hif.com.au/mental-health/the-importance-of-seeking-help

Harvard Health. (2022, January 10). *What causes depression?* Retrieved May 26, 2022, from https://www.health.harvard.edu/mind-and-mood/what-causes-depression

Herrick, K. (2019, November 7). *Toddler-Proof Your Phone: Tips, Tricks & Recommendations*. ASecureLife.Com. Retrieved April 18, 2022, from https://www.asecurelife.com/toddler-proof-your-phone/

Holland, K. (2021, October 21). *Childhood Emotional Neglect: How It Can Impact You Now and Later*. Healthline. Retrieved May 4, 2022, from https://www.healthline.com/health/mental-health/childhood-emotional-neglects

Jacobs, C. (2020, July 17). *Share The Parenting Load: 5 Ways To Do It Well*. Smaggle. Retrieved May 16, 2022, from https://www.smaggle.com/share-the-parenting-load-5-ways-to-do-it/

Kriz, D. (2020, July 20). *8 Keys to Accepting Things that Are Out of Your Control –*. Foundations Counseling. Retrieved May 31, 2022, from https://www.yournewfoundation.com/8-keys-to-accepting-things-that-are-out-of-your-control/

Marshall, C. (2019, December 11). *17 mistakes every first time dad will make*. Metro. Retrieved April 16, 2022, from https://metro.co.uk/2015/04/18/17-mistakes-every-first-time-dad-will-make-5154750/

MasterClass staff. (2021, August 19). *How to Improve Your Research Skills: 6 Research Tips*. MasterClass. Retrieved April 18, 2022, from https://www.masterclass.com/articles/how-to-improve-your-research-skills#quiz-0

Mayo Clinic Staff. (2021, April 21). *Crying baby? How to keep your cool*. Mayo Clinic. Retrieved April 13, 2022, from https://www.mayoclinic.org/healthy-lifestyle/infant-and-toddler-health/in-depth/crying-baby/art-20046995?reDate=13042022

McGuinness, D. (2022). *9 Common Baby Care Myths Debunked*. MemorialCare. Retrieved April 16, 2022, from https://www.memorialcare.org/blog/9-common-baby-care-myths-debunked

Mental Health Foundation. (2018, June 15). *Top 5 tips by dads, for dads, on looking after mental health*. Retrieved May 17, 2022, from https://www.mentalhealth.org.uk/blog/top-5-tips-dads-dads-looking-after-mental-health

Miller, W. (2021, December 22). *How to Deal When Your Ex Wants to Be the "Fun" Parent*. Medium. Retrieved April 19, 2022, from https://medium.com/modern-parent/how-to-deal-when-your-ex-wants-to-be-the-fun-parent-d365878cee93

Naidoo, U., MD. (2019, March 27). *Gut feelings: How food affects your mood*. Harvard Health. Retrieved May 2, 2022, from https://www.health.harvard.edu/blog/gut-feelings-how-food-affects-your-mood-2018120715548.

NCT. 2019. "Diarrhoea and Vomiting in Babies." NCT (National Childbirth Trust). July 11, 2019. https://www.nct.org.uk/baby-toddler/your-babys-health/what-watch-out-for/diarrhoea-and-vomiting-babies.

"NPR Choice Page." 2019. Npr.org. 2019. https://www.npr.org/sections/health-shots/2016/04/05/473002684/for-new-parents-dad-may-be-the-one-missing-the-most-sleep.

Null, J. (2022, March 4). *No Heat Stroke*. NoHeatStroke. Retrieved April 18, 2022, from https://www.noheatstroke.org/

Our Family Wizard. (2021, January 8). *Back to School: Keeping Both Parents Involved*. OurFamilyWizard. Retrieved May 16, 2022, from https://www.ourfamilywizard.com/blog/back-to-school-keeping-both-parents-involved

Parents Editors. (2009, June 8). *10 Surprising Safety Hazards*. Parents. Retrieved June 6, 2022, from https://www.parents.com/baby/safety/babyproofing/safety-hazards/

Parker, W. (2022, January 13). *How Divorced Fathers Can Still Be Successful Parents*. Verywell Family. Retrieved May 16, 2022, from https://www.verywellfamily.com/tips-to-succeed-as-a-co-parenting-father-4129032

Peate, I. (2020, February 10). *Call for evidence for new plan to improve mental health*. Independent Nurse. Retrieved April 18, 2022, from https://www.independentnurse.co.uk/clinical-article/does-anyone-ask-new-dads-how-they-are-feeling/223989/

Pous, T. (2019, January 11). *17 Pieces Of Advice For New Dads That Are Actually Really Helpful*. BuzzFeed. Retrieved April 17, 2022, from https://www.buzzfeed.com/terripous/advice-for-new-dads

Pous, Terri. 2018. "17 Pieces of Advice for New Dads That Are Actually Really Helpful." BuzzFeed. June 14, 2018. Accessed April 9, 2022. https://www.buzzfeed.com/terripous/advice-for-new-dads.

Reese, N. (2019, July 3). *10 Simple Ways to Relieve Stress*. Healthline. Retrieved April 13, 2022, from https://www.healthline.-com/health/10-ways-to-relieve-stress

Relate. (2022). *How to maintain a healthy relationship after a baby has been born | Relate*. Relate The Relationship People. Retrieved May 16, 2022, from https://www.relate.org.uk/relationship-help/help-family-life-and-parenting/new-parents/how-maintain-healthy-relationship-after-baby-has-been-born

RL360. (2022). *Top 10 financial tips for new dads this father's day | RL360 Top 10*. Retrieved April 16, 2022, from https://www.r-l360.com/top10/financial-tips-for-new-dads.htm

Seguss, J. (2015, July 14). *Readers Reveal: Surprising Ways Life Changes When You Become a Parent*. Parents. Retrieved April 18, 2022, from https://www.parents.com/pregnancy/considering-baby/is-it-time/life-changes-after-baby/

Seven Awesome Tips for New Dads." 2014. HuffPost UK. July 15, 2014. https://www.huffingtonpost.co.uk/torsten-klaus/advice-for-new-dads_b_5585315.html

Shadwell, T. (2020, October 5). *Five-month-old baby killed by van after mum forgets to put brakes on runaway pram*. Mirror. Retrieved April 18, 2022, from https://www.mirror.co.uk/news/world-news/five-month-old-baby-killed-22795596

Shapin, A. (2019, December 16). *Why We Need to Stop the Comparison Game*. The Everymom. Retrieved April 17, 2022, from https://theev erymom.com/why-we-need-to-stop-the-comparison-game/

Shaw, A. (2015, July 15). *My worst flaw as a father: How a 'good parent' can still be a jerk*. InstaFather | New Parent Guidance and Support. Retrieved April 13, 2022, from https://www.instafather.com/dad-blog/2015/7/13/my-worst-flaw-as-a-father-how-a-good-parent-can-still-be-a-jerk

Shaw, A. (2018, November 7). *3 scary mistakes new dads need to avoid with babies*. InstaFather | New Parent Guidance and Support. Retrieved April 18, 2022, from https://www.instafather.com/dad-blog/2015/8/2/the-one-thing-you-absolutely-cannot-do-as-a-new-dad

Shaw, J. (2019, July 19). *9 Common Mistakes Dads Make*. Positively Dad. Retrieved April 18, 2022, from https://positivelydad.com/9-common-mistakes-dads-make/

Sole-Smith, V. (2018, August 20). *How to Share the Parenting Load With Your Partner*. Parents. Retrieved May 16, 2022, from https://www.parents.com/parenting/better-parenting/advice/ways-to-share-the-parenting-load-with-your-partner/

Taylor, M. (2020, January 16). *Benefits Of Hiring A Babysitter (42 Unexpected Advantages)*. Kidsit Babysitting Tips. Retrieved April 18, 2022, from https://kidsit.com/benefits-of-hiring-a-babysitter

US Department of Health and Human Services. (2021, April 21). *Data and Statistics for SIDS and SUID | CDC*. CDC. Retrieved April 18, 2022, from https://www.cdc.gov/sids/data.htm

User Melbournemum2014. (2015, April 8). *Forgot the pram brake.* Babycenter. Retrieved April 18, 2022, from https://www.babycen ter.com.au/thread/1675417/forgot-the-pram-brake

Vann, C. (2017, July 22). *Overly Strict Parenting Causing Long-Term Psychological Consequences: Experts.* VOA Cambodia. Retrieved April 18, 2022, from https://www.voacambodia.com/a/overly-strict-parenting-causing-long-term-psychological-consequences-say-experts/3953896.html#:~:text=Those%20with%20strict%%2020-parents%20and,change%20their%20way%20of%20thi%20nking

Venkateshwar, V., & Raghu Raman, T. S. (2017, July 10). *Failure to Thrive.* National Library of Medicine. Retrieved June 2, 2022, from https://www.ncbi.nlm.nih.gov/pmc/articles/PMC5532051/

Villines, Z. (2015, March 27). *Are Men More Likely Than Women to Want Kids? And Other News.* GoodTherapy.Org Therapy Blog. Retrieved May 9, 2022, from https://www.goodtherapy.org/blog/are-men-more-likely-than-women-to-want-kids-and-other-news-0327151

"Vomiting in Babies: What's Normal and What's Not." 2018. BabyCentre UK. 2018. https://www.babycentre.-co.uk/a536689/vomiting-in-babies-whats-normal-and-whats-not

Wehrli, Ashley. 2017. "Dangers of Not Changing the Baby's Diaper Fast Enough | BabyGaga." BabyGaga. BabyGaga. August 31, 2017. https://www.babygaga.com/15-dangers-of-not-changing-the-babys-diaper-fast-enough/

Weiss, R. E. (2021, June 14). *Benefits of Rooming In With Your Baby After Birth.* Verywell Family. Retrieved April 17, 2022, from https://www.verywellfamily.com/benefits-of-rooming-in-with-your-baby-2758930

Welch, N. (2012, June 4). *Celebrate Father's Day by avoiding the top 5 mistakes new Dads make.* New Parent - Essential Guide for New Parents, Moms, and Baby Products. Retrieved April 18, 2022, from https://newparent.com/mom/celebrate-fathers-day-by-avoiding-the-top-5-mistakes-new-dads-make1/

White, J. (2020, May 7). *How to Respond When People Criticize Your Parenting.* Verywell Family. Retrieved April 13, 2022, from https://www.verywellfamily.com/when-people-judge-your-parenting-style-284540

Woodrum, M. (2022, January 7). *But Everyone Makes Mistakes - A Parent Is Born.* Medium. Retrieved May 17, 2022, from https://medium.com/a-parent-is-born/but-everyone-makes-mistakes-ca709e14a120

Zmuda, E. (2015, October 8). *Top 12 Tips to Give Relatives who are Babysitting for the First Time.* Nation Wide Children's. Retrieved April 18, 2022, from https://www.nationwidechildrens.org/family-resources-education/700childrens/2015/10/top-12-tips-to-give-relatives-who-are-babysitting-for-the-first-time

Printed in Great Britain
by Amazon

12210310R00108